TO DIE BEFORE DEATH
The Sufi Way of Life

by

M. R. Bawa Muhaiyaddeen

THE FELLOWSHIP PRESS
Philadelphia, Pennsylvania

On the cover is a painting by Denise Sati Barnett depicting "The Tree of Souls" as described on pages 99-101. Each light on this tree in paradise represents the light of a soul on earth. When a light fades, it means a life is ending, and the Angel of Death must go and retrieve that soul.

Library of Congress Cataloging-in-Publication Data

Muhaiyaddeen, M. R. Bawa
   To Die Before Death:The Sufi Way of Life
by M. R. Bawa Muhaiyaddeen.
            p. cm.
   Includes index.
   ISBN 0-914390-37-6   ISBN 0-914390-39-2 (pbk.)
   1. Sufism I. Title
BP189. M694 1996
297'.23—dc20   94-4745
                                        CIP

Printed in the United States of America
by The Fellowship Press
Bawa Muhaiyaddeen Fellowship
1st Printing 1997
2nd Printing 2003

Muhammad Raheem Bawa Muhaiyaddeen ☺

CONTENTS

INTRODUCTION

———— ··◁∞▷·· ————

A Sufi said: "And on That Day He will have the oysters tossed onto the shore; He will open each one to find which ones grew a pearl."

In the name of God who is forever bestowing infinite love, compassion, and mercy upon us, may all who read this book be blessed with the wisdom of the tranquil heart, the heart that rests in the knowledge of God's goodness. The comfort of wisdom cannot be measured; its fruit is pure faith, service, and loving kindness. The author of this book exemplified these traits with every gesture of his life, and his teaching continues to awaken these traits in those who seek with sincerity and wisdom.

Death has a sudden sting to it. Life's dramas are stripped bare of their glitter. The only real consolation is in the wisdom that knows the One of infinite mercy and love, the One power we call God. The spontaneous discourses that comprise this book emanated from a man liberated from mind and desire who fully conquered ignorance. The meanings in these teachings can help provide the guidance which awakens the wisdom to really know. May each of us be blessed with the wisdom that knows the presence of God, may we overcome all fears of our own dying, be comforted in knowing that those who have gone before us are in the hands of the Most Merciful, and live each moment with the appreciation of its being a gift. May we live with hearts full of love and the courage to treat all lives with that love. The author of this book provides us with proof that a human

being can attain absorption in God and live without selfishness continually demonstrating God's divine qualities. May
each of us come to understand the magnitude of God's grace
and realize the miracle of becoming true human beings.

M. R. Bawa Muhaiyaddeen (Ral.), may God's infinite
love and blessings forever be poured upon him, ceased
serving with his body on December 8, 1986. As a fully
realized person, he lived that of which he spoke. He treated
all lives as his own life and his own life proved the reality
that a human being can be annihilated in God. For over forty
years, of which we know, he lived in Sri Lanka, where, after
having been discovered by pilgrims in the Kataragama
forests, he served the wisdom that arises from intimacy with
the Divine to people of all races, classes, and religions
without distinction. In his ashram in Jaffna, I once observed
tears fall from a deer's eyes while he sang a song; I cannot
put a limit on the community of lives which he serves.

He spoke Tamil, an ancient Dravidian language of
South Asia, and Tamil people call him a *gnāni*, a sage who
has attained divine luminous wisdom, and Muslims refer to
him as a Sufi.[1] Yet, he is beyond any labels, as a father to all
lives and at the same time as the humblest of all people. He
often referred to himself as a small ant man.[2]

He did many extraordinary things. For example, by
himself he cleared nineteen acres of jungle and created a
farm, demonstrating a model for success to very poor villag-
ers, and then he gave the farm away to those who worked it.

In 1971 he came to America to revive the remembrance
of the true human station: "Man lives within God; God lives
within man.[3] God is man's secret; man is God's secret. God is
man's treasury; man is God's treasury." Realizing this state of
unity with God who is complete and infinite love[4] is the
purpose of our lives.

Our human potential, that which he called true man, is

eternal, formless, genderless, beyond race, religion, philosophy, and concepts of any kind. It is a plenitude of goodness beyond description. It is the very light of consciousness itself. Within the discovery of this subtle wondrous treasure (nūtpamāna porul) within oneself is the discovery of heaven. "You will observe that within yourself that heaven exists. And it is within yourself that your evolutionary birth (pirappu) and your future birth is immanent, and it is such knowledge that you must strive to find out, to know and understand, and this is obligatory on you." M. R. Bawa Muhaiyaddeen, *Wisdom of the Divine*, Vol. 2, p. 65.

There are prerequisites for entering into these profound experiences to which Bawa Muhaiyaddeen (Ral.) is beckoning. For example, he stated in no uncertain terms the precondition of universal love: "Without first having established love for mankind, one cannot establish love of God."[5]

Why a book regarding death? It is a mystery of paramount impact. Death helps explain the meaning of what we do in our lives. Its finality places our intentions, our thoughts, and our deeds in context. If we reflect on it thoroughly, the significance of each moment becomes known. We can choose to live in a shallow manner. We can choose to live deeply with sincerity of purpose. We can choose to follow mind and desire; we can choose to affirm God's presence through compassion, love, kindness, patience, and justice. When the profound value of each moment is measured we can say "Yes" to life, affirming God's gift with our entire being. A heart complete with such gratitude can receive the wisdom that penetrates the veils of mystery.

When a loved one passes on, we reflect on how their life will be evaluated by the One Judge. If we have any intelligence we will reflect on how our lives must now be analyzed, how we must begin the process of evaluating now. We can remember our own death or we can live pretending

it will not happen. This book is for those who want to see
without fear, without veils, without illusions. It is for those
who want to affirm God's beneficence and live with hearts of
gratitude. This book is for those who want to awaken completely and know the Lord.

An aspect of living realization is to allow the attachment to everything that changes, everything that dies, to fall
away in the absorption of love for God. First is the analysis
of who one is and then the letting go, the surrender of all
that does not exist eternally.[6] This process reveals the imperishable aspect of our life, and it is beautiful beyond words
and symbols, such as those found in scriptures, art, or even
creation.[7] The kingdom of heaven is inside us and that is part
of the "good news" each Prophet of God has brought us.

When a person finds this incomparable and irresistible
treasure, the brilliant beauty of the heart (aham) merges with
the countenance[8] of the splendor of God's glory (muham). This
station of merging can be understood as Muhammad (Sal.).[9]
At this station the deep meaning of sacred language is
revealed.

Without in any way diminishing the value of the mercy
of God found in the aspects of external guidance found in
holy scriptures such as the Bible, Hindu Puranas, the Zend-
Avesta, the Torah, and the Qur'an,[10] and places of pilgrimage
and worship, it is necessary to point out that Sufis use language in a unique and profoundly charged manner designed
to awaken the inner infinite dimensions of life. In order to
cause an awakening from the slumber of the limits of mind
and desire, words are used to sharply prod us to higher levels
of attainment. These are some of the author's previous
explanations of key terms found in this book.

Sufism: "Sufism occurs when the 'I' is destroyed[11]...Sufis
came even before the time of the Rasūl (Sal.), at the time of

Adam (A.S.). When the self has disappeared, when the mind
and desire are dispelled, when the self is forgotten, when
God is held as one's own life, one's body, when one's actions
and behavior and qualities are as God's, that is what is called
Sufi. And that state comes gradually, it grows gradually...A
Sufi sees only the ideals of wisdom. He becomes the mirror.[12] His heart becomes the mirror. So he does not see
himself. Wisdom is what he sees. Audio cassette: M. R. Bawa
Muhaiyaddeen, *What is Sufism?*, November 13, 1983.[13]

Islam: "It is for *Īmān* (Certitude) that we use the label
Islam and not for anything else. To him in whom Certitude
(*Īmān*-Faith) is founded with that supreme conviction of the
all-pervading Oneness of God, the Supreme Creator, the
Omniscient, the Eternal, the Self-Subsisting, without friend
or supporter, the Master of all creation, the Lord (Allah),
that He alone exists—to him who only sees Him and Him
alone with the eye of the heart (*Qalb*) and is blinded to all
other things, who is impervious to all other things, who is
strengthened with the determination and radiance of that
Certitude (*Īmān*-Faith)...**to whatsoever religion he may
belong and whomsoever he may be, who possesses such a
Qalb (Heart) in which such Certitude (*Īmān*-Faith) is
ingrained, it is he who is Islam.** The term Islam is applicable
only to that particular state of being, an innate quality...It is
in essence, the Purest of the Pure—so much like a polished
crystal which is free of even an atom of dirt—so much so,
that within the radiant Purity of that Certitude (*Īmān*) we
find that faculty to see Him, as well as all that is of the Finite
and Infinite (*kullum yāvum*) in their Eternal Beauty. This is
called Islam." M. R. Bawa Muhaiyaddeen, *Wisdom of the Divine*,
Vol. 1, p. 72.

"*Īmān-Islām* refers to that state of being when one never
hurts nor kills the life of another in any way whatsoever, a
state in which neither the hearts nor the lives of other beings

are harmed." *Wisdom of the Divine*, Vol. 3, p. 54. "And every conceivable life form is a supreme expression of that essential Purity (*Parisuthamāna*) which may also be described by another term, Islam; and without which life in any physical vehicle is not manifest." (The term Islam in this sense does not refer to any particular religious group or creed.) M. R. Bawa Muhaiyaddeen, *Wisdom of the Divine*, Vol. 2, p. 9.

Qur'an: The Qur'an has descended to that Effulgence of the Essence (*Dhāt*), the Light onto the Light of the Essence (*Dhāt*) which is called 'Muhammad'. M. R. Bawa Muhaiyaddeen, *Wisdom of the Divine*, Vol. 3, p. 57. Qur'an is a station of communion with God. See M. R. Bawa Muhaiyaddeen, *Wisdom of the Divine*, Vol. 3, p. 58. See also *Golden Words of a Sufi Sheikh*, p. 17.

Ka'bah: "[T]he real Ka'bah of the Almighty is the heart (*qalb*) of man (*insān*)." M. R. Bawa Muhaiyaddeen, *Wisdom of the Divine*, Vol. 2, p. 10. "...our Heart (*qalb*) is the Ka'bah within us, the Station or Throne where God (Allah) Himself reposes. It is therefore the House of God (Allah) within us. Within this most excellent (*sirandha*) repository, the Perfect being (*Niraintha Porul*) is evident, together with the divine secrets (*Sirr*), divine attributes (*Sifāt*), beauty (*Alahu*), contentment, pleasure and pain, heaven and hell, good and evil, darkness and light, illusion and the light of Truth...the mysteries of the 18,000 universes... M. R. Bawa Muhaiyaddeen, *Wisdom of the Divine*, Vol. 1, p. 46. "This then is our inner Ka'bah, which is utterly unlike the Ka'bah of brick and mortar, or even of any temple, church, or mosque built by man. *Ibid.* p. 48.

To Die Before Death: "An individual who has no burden—nothing, is free because his ego—the 'I' has died with its complement, the *Nafs* (worldly desires). And it is such an individual who develops the awareness that just beyond, only He exists; he came, he learnt his lesson, he realized that there is nothing he could carry away with him when his time came, so that he carries nothing, and he is nothing, and therefore he is in a position to see Him, like a racehorse running a race from the starting point, and comes back to that point knowing that the race is over, and awaits its reward on winning the race. A burdened horse cannot run swiftly, and surely, it cannot win a race. And such is the difference, the distinction between *Hayāt* or Life and *Maut* or Death. If we run our own race in this fashion, and eliminate the 'Ego' or the 'I' factor during our life on earth we say that we have gained tangibly, and we may be said to have 'died before death'." M. R. Bawa Muhaiyaddeen, *Wisdom of the Divine*, Vol. 1, pp. 40-41.

For a person who has realized this Muhammad (Sal.), entered this Ka'bah, read this Qur'an, and died before death, who is there to be judged in this life or afterwards? What becomes of their existence? How do they express gratitude to and praise of God?

Bawa Muhaiyaddeen (Ral.) demonstrated that for one who has realized God, there exists only selfless service. For this reason he lived as a slave to God, serving all lives as his own. This station of serving all lives with the divine qualities contains a secret. "God is the King to the king, the Most Powerful to the powerful, and He is the Servant to His servants and the Slave to His slaves."

Yet, Bawa Muhaiyaddeen (Ral.) used to call himself a student and he continually exhorted those around him to always remain students. I asked him one afternoon, "How can you call yourself a student, having obtained the light of wisdom and being merged in God?"

He answered that if one threw a stone into a still pond the ripples would expand outward. He said that when a man throws his heart (*qalb*) completely into the heart (*qalb*) of God that learning is then from within the expanding resonance of God's compassion.

At that moment, and such is the power of words of wisdom, I experienced the expansion of the Guide, the Master, seeking God within and through me, and the recognition that this seeking is occurring through each life, that all lives are seeking reunion with God. It is this questing deep in each heart and soul that causes the attraction to truth.[14] A purpose of our birth, a purpose of creation, is to fulfill this seeking.

Coming to know ourselves is fulfilling God's purpose. Two *Abādīth* are relevant: "He who knows himself, knows his Lord"; and, "I (Allah) was a hidden treasure: I loved (*hubb*) to be known. Hence, I created the world so that I would be known." Our coming to truly understand the full dimensions of our humanity is fulfilling God's loving purpose.

The Guide for this knowing is the Light that emerges from the qualities of goodness. This is called *Nūr Muhammad*.[15] That which explains the meanings and wonders in this awakened state is the *Qutb*. This knowing expands within love itself. As we awaken from the dream of ignorance the Light of Knowledge radiates. It radiates through each of our hearts as our wisdom dawns. It knows itself through us. This light and this axis of life are the resonance of God. God seeks God; God comes to know God.

He is realizing Himself through each soul which comes to know itself. This is the purpose of this book, to help us know the most important part of our lives, who we really are, the essence of our being, the One Eternal Self, closer than our veins and the only power that sustains us. There is immeasurable peace in knowing our indivisible intimacy with God. Who will not know peace who knows the One of Unbounded Love? It is to know the blessing of this revelation: "O soul at peace, return to thy Lord, well pleased, well-pleasing! Enter thou among My servants! Enter thou My Paradise!" Qur'an 89:27-30.

The *Qutb* who guides this knowing cannot perish and his physical presence is not required for us to receive his guidance. A heart melted with caring for all lives as one's own is required. He is the intimate student within the heart. Allah is the Seeker seeking Himself. He is the Knower loving to be known. That will be experienced as eternal Light. Then you will know you do not die. Then you will know what is meant when we speak of the Prophets, the *Qutb, Muhaiyaddeen*, your true self and the author of this book. Then you will know the relationship each has with God, the perfect never-ending relationship of true love, forgiveness, mercy, kindness, and in surrender, bliss beyond description. Some may know of this. May all of us, with the grace of the beneficent One who has created us, who is blessing us with the beating of our hearts, the gift of this very next breath, may that One who creates, sustains, and absorbs our lives, grant us purity, lives of freedom, and lives of knowing and selfless service that bring comfort to all. *Amīn.*

Respectfully submitted by one upon whom a small drop of grace has mercifully fallen, and who remains forever grateful for His kindness.

Ahamed Muhaiyaddeen

FOOTNOTES

1. "Sufi is a unique word...It does not relate to any particular religion. It belongs to all of humanity...Sufi is a clear, pure Essence that has filtered and settled slowly, deep within. It goes beyond the state of *mounam* (silence), even beyond the station of the *mouna guru* (the silent guru within

us). It is that State of Stillness when the Resplendence of the Pure Clarity of Wisdom has sunk down and settled completely within its ultimate Completeness and Perfection...It is not something that belongs to any one religion. It is the Essence which has been filtered out from all four religions by Wisdom...(It) is to bestow Love, Kindness, Compassion, and Mercy on all creations...He does not acknowledge differences of races, religions or any separations. He embraces only God, His 3,000 Gracious Qualities, and His Plenitude. One who has attained this State is Sufi. One who has known and realized this state of: *Lā ilāha*, nothing other than God exists; *ill-Allāhu*, You alone are God. This is Sufi...One who loses himself into nothingness, where the state of the self does not exist; one who knows the station where only God remains as that Solitary Oneness that is God: this is the explanation of Sufi." Excerpts from a pamphlet published by and available from The Bawa Muhaiyaddeen Fellowship titled "SUFI."

2. "In all God's creation, I am a very, very small man. I am a small, little ant man." Unpublished talk of July 31, 1973 cassette tape available from The Bawa Muhaiyaddeen Fellowship titled "Ant Man." Also recommended tape of November 2, 1975 titled "Ants and Sufism" in which Bawa Muhaiyaddeen exhorts seekers to remain humble and small to avoid spiritual pitfalls.

3. Bawa Muhaiyaddeen (Ral.) considered this aphorism so significant that asserting it as a corporate purpose is contained in the first article of the Articles of Incorporation of The Bawa Muhaiyaddeen Fellowship that he established in Philadelphia, PA. On the occasion of the 15th Anniversary Celebration of his United States arrival, he stated, "God is within man and man is within God. This is the secret of life. Understanding this is the meaning of man's life. This is true devotion to God. This is what dispels the darkness and

makes man resplendent. Once man understands this, there
will be no differences. He will realize the entire human
generation as one and God as One. *Āmīn.*"

4. The Divine Perfections are God's Beautiful Names.
As the Qur'an says: "The most beautiful names are God's."
7:180 "God, there is no divinity but He; to Him belong the
most beautiful names." 20:8 "Invoke God or invoke the
Merciful; by whatever name you invoke Him, the most
beautiful names are His." 17:110.

5. From an interview with Robert Muller, Chancellor of
the University of Peace and Former Assistant Secretary-
General of the United Nations, August 20, 1984 (tape
available). Bawa Muhaiyaddeen (Ral.) clearly meant the most
universal non-sectarian, all-encompassing love as he stated in
the talk in discussing the necessity of ending religious pride,
differences, and prejudice: "Religions are the cause of murder, wars, evil, differences, and discrimination. If only man
would reflect and say that religion is common to all. All four
religions are from the same tree and all that is wanted is the
taste of the fruit. It does not matter what name we call it. If
man can realize this, there will be no war and no bitterness.
My brother, this is the biggest problem that faces the world
today. How many murders, how many wars, how many lives
are lost in vain in battles of racial and religious differences?"
Also, note as a precondition of true faith the *Hadīth* of
Muhammad (Sal.): "Not one of you will believe until he
loves for his brother that which he loves for himself." For
Bawa Muhaiyaddeen (Ral.) all real love should lead to God's
selfless love. "When we look at love, we see only His love."
M. R. Bawa Muhaiyaddeen (Ral.), *Book of God's Love*, p. 18.

6. "Everything is perishable except His Face." Qur'an
28:88; "All that dwells upon earth is perishing, yet still abides
the Face of the Lord, majestic, splendid." Qur'an 55:26-27.

7. From the point of wisdom everything is a lesson, a metaphor, an example; God is the only reality. The body and all of creation itself is symbolic, a grand story containing and revealing the mystery of God's wonders such that He may become known. Bawa Muhaiyaddeen (Ral.) has explained that the human form can be represented by 28 symbols (*Acharam* in Tamil or the 28 letters of the Arabic alphabet depending on which metaphor he is using) each one being an expression of the divine secret. Additionally, he has explained that anatomically, there is a piece of flesh, a node on the right side of the heart, next to the lung called the *Bismin kāi*. It can also be understood as a mystical term referring to the imperishable within the perishable; it represents the indestructible "place" where faith is strengthened and where the *dhikr*, remembrance of God, is established. In esoteric symbology it is where Jibrīl (Angel Gabriel) (A.S.) is located, as each major angel is symbolically referred to as an organ. Within it is a point, a power, a place where light dwells. It is God's house where He has placed wisdom, the *alif*, the *qutbiyyat* (the sixth level of consciousness which explains the truth of God), and everything else within it. On the Day of Questioning it is through this point that we are raised up. Clearly, there is a deep mystery in this term.

8. "Withersoever you turn, there is the Face of God." Qur'an 2:115. His immanence is emphasized again in Qur'an, 50:16, "We are nearer to him (man) than the jugular vein."

9. See M. R. Bawa Muhaiyaddeen, *Wisdom of the Divine*, Vol. 3, pp. 53, 55, 59 and M. R. Bawa Muhaiyaddeen, *The Guidebook to the True Secret of the Heart*, Vol. 1, p. 221. Clearly the term Muhammad in this context is referring to a state of wisdom. In the text of this book, *To Die Before Death: The Sufi Way of Life*, the author uses the term with parallel meanings, multi-level meanings, sometimes referring only to the state

of realization and sometimes referring only to the temporal man. (Sal.) is the abbreviation of *Sallallāhu 'alaihi wa sallam*, God bless him and grant him peace. Sal. is placed after Muhammad in every instance in this book, in the interest of respect for one of the Holy Prophets of God and in an effort not to interject the editor's interpretation of which aspect the author intended each time the term is used.

10. "[A]ll these scriptures contain the words of grace given by God to the prophets. That grace is light. If you look at these scriptures on the outside you will see only a book, nothing more. If you look inside the cover, you will find pages, letters, words, sentences, and stories. But if you look deep within, you will find Allah, the words of Allah, the duties of the prophets, the commandments, the power, and the light." M. R. Bawa Muhaiyaddeen, *Islam and World Peace*, p. 38.

11. "Noah said: 'O unbelievers, I am not I,

I am dead and God is alive.'

When the 'I' is dead in the senses of man,

The speaker, the hearer, the knower is God.

When the 'I' is not 'I', then the 'I' is the breath of God.

To challenge Him is a mistake."

Jalaladeen Rumi's *Mathnawi*.

In Genesis 5:24 it states that the Prophet Enoch "walked with God, and he was not, for God took him." In much Sufi expression there are different stages of *fanā'*, annihilation, and it is often stated that after one is *fanā'* (annihilated) God can make that person *baqā'* (remaining in permanence) in Himself, in a sense walking with God. Another understanding could be the distinction between a sponge being tossed into the ocean becoming saturated with the water and a glass of water being tossed into the ocean and merging entirely. I believe it is the latter expression Bawa Muhaiyaddeen (Ral.) means regarding *fanā'*, since it was that state of inseparable absorption that we observed in his life. He proved the reality of this exalted state.

12. The relationship with a person who has become such a mirror is unique. Tremendous love and devotion is engendered. Yet, it is not for the mirror, the man, but for the beauty of God that they are able to reflect. Truly wise people are able to turn our attention toward God—the One Life within our very lives.

13. This audio tape is available through The Bawa Muhaiyaddeen Fellowship, Audio Department, 5820 Overbrook Avenue, Philadelphia, PA 19131 as are most of the talks in this book. There are hundreds of discourses by the author available in audio casssette and many on video tape.

14. This attraction to the light of truth is one of the meanings of being a follower of Muhammad (Sal.). Living with pure faith in God can be understood as being in the tribe of Abraham (A.S.). May God's Peace be upon him. Knowing that the entire human family is one, arising from one mother and father is understanding our common heritage in Adam and Eve (A.S.).

15. See *Questions of Life—Answers of Wisdom*, p. 289.

PART ONE

To Die Before Death

THE FINAL SUMMONS

*B*efore the closing and opening of an eye,
Within the blinking of an eye,
Within the blinking of an eye
We will be called back
    to the compassionate feet of God.
As the atom within the atom within the atom,
In the most subtle way He will call us back.
How can we describe His subtle ways, His final call!
How can we describe the wonder
With which He sends His final summons!

All our life He made us grow and grow and grow.
As the days went by and as more days went by,
We lived on in this life without doing any good,
Right to the end,
Drenched in sorrow and suffering,
In laughter and happiness.
The sorrow in our life and the suffering,
The good and the bad that come through blood ties,
All the sorrows that come connected with this birth
    of ours,
All the sorrows and sufferings that collected within us
Make our life one of suffering and grief
With tears, weeping, and laughter.

3

Yet, having grown in this way,

Even at the end when we can bear no more,

When death comes to summon us,

When it says, "Come,"

And within a second takes us along,

When it gives that call,

So subtle, so brisk, so quick,

We still do not realize this!

We go on believing that this world is vast,

Thinking all kinds of unthinkable thoughts,

That this world is ours,

That this world is a treasure.

Giving up all the things that we accumulated,

Throwing them into the streets,

Weeping and in dire straits,

We must open our mouth and call to our Father,

Bow to His divine feet,

And go toward Him.

Then He will summon us.

Forgetting everything else and remembering
   only Him,

We must go toward Him.

On that day, all our sorrows will be dispelled.

Then happiness and the grace of God

And His love will come to embrace us,

Bringing us peace and tranquility.

They will come and embrace us on that day

And that will be true peace.

All the states that existed up until then,

All that we gathered, collected, and used

Were only bundles of sin and nothing more.

All of them were the evils and sins we had gathered.

All the things that we gathered in ignorance

Were merely sacks and bundles of evil.

If we can throw away all the bundles of ignorance
    that we have gathered,

If we can dispel all our evils,

If we can look for the divine feet of God,

God who is One,

The One with love,

In whom we must place our faith and trust,

If we can bow at His feet,

Surrender to Him and pay obeisance to Him,

Only then will we have peace and tranquility.

That will be justice and truth.

When certitude in Him and worship of Him

Come to dwell within us,

When they are established within us

And we trust in that All-Powerful, All-Pervasive God,

Then we will be in the state to show peace
    and tranquility to all lives.

We must always live our life with faith
    in that One God.
O my child, we must live forever in that faith.
Just as the trees that bear ripe fruit
Share their fruit with everyone,
All the things that we gather in our life
We must share.
All the things we accumulate,
All the benefits we acquire in our life,
This heart must share with everyone,
Just as the tree shares its ripe fruit.
Then we will have peace,
And we will have tranquility.
When the tree gives away its fruit, it knows peace.
And if our mind gives away all that it has,
Then it, too, will know peace.
Let us find this state of equality.
That will be the best way for our life.
That will be best for us.
Āmīn. Āmīn.
I give you my love.

September 24, 1985

1

Destiny

———————⟨∞⟩——————

M ay God protect us from the qualities of satan, the rejected one. May God protect us from satan, the rejected one. *A'ūdhu billāhi minash-shaitānir-rajīm.* O God, O God, *Yā Allāh.* O Merciful One, O Merciful One, *Yā Rahmān.* O Compassionate One, O Compassionate One, *Yā Rahīm.* O Ruler of the universes, O Ruler of the universes, *Yā Rabbal-'ālamīn.*

O Merciful One who rules over everything in this world *('ālam)* and the world of the souls *(arwāh)*, the Leader of everything, the Foremost One who sustains everything, the Lord who created everything, You created everything with Your grace and Your wealth. The things that You created are very intricate. You have created things that are supremely technical. No one else could have done the research or work that You have done. Everything You did was a novel, wondrous research. You investigated currents, magnetic forces, and all other forces, atom by atom. You are the only One who did the research and created everything. You are the Lord, the *Rabb.* You know what can be grown where, what can burn what, and what can control what. You are *Allāhu,* the One of unfathomable grace and incomparable love, the bestower of the undiminishing wealth of grace. You are the Lord of all the universes. This is why we praise You.

You have all the power and all the benevolence to create, to fashion, to destroy, and to protect. You know what to protect, what to embrace, and what to destroy. You are the One of perfect purity. You will protect everything that is

7

perfectly pure and destroy everything that is impure and
does not join with You. You will take everything that is
valuable and discard everything that is of no value. Among
all the forces (shaktis), You will take the forces that are right
and not the ones that are improper. You are the Foremost
One of might and exaltedness, O Lord of the universes. This
is why all lives pray to You. There is no doubt that You can
do everything. We believe this.

Anyone who has wisdom, anyone who has absolute
faith, certitude, and determination (īmān), anyone who has
trust in You, anyone who has even a little sense, even a little
awareness, will not forget You. Only if a person is fascinated
by the world will he forget You. The fascination of the world
and the qualities of satan will make a person forget You.
Only a person who has the arrogance of satan will forget
You; otherwise he will never forget You.

Such arrogance takes possession of man and causes
changes to occur. O God, please correct such people and
show them Your compassion. Give them compassionate
hearts, destroy their pride, and give them qualities of peace
and tranquility. Destroy the quality that says, "I," and give
them the quality that says, "We." Destroy the quality that
says, "Mine!" and give them the quality that says,
"Everyone's." Make them give up their anger and give them
patience. Make them give up the quality of saying, "I, I, I!"
and give them the peacefulness of saying, "We, we, we."
Make them give up thinking, "My property, my land, my
forest, my country," and let them realize that this is God's
kingdom.

Everything belongs to God—ourselves, our lives, our
bodies—everything belongs to God. When we ourselves
belong to Him, how can anything belong to us? The only
thing that belongs to us is God. Please give us the clarity and
the wisdom to realize completely that our only wealth is

God. Please give us, who are of the human race, this clarity,
give other lives the appropriate qualities and wisdom, and
protect us so that we may understand You.

O God, who can fully describe Your greatness! You are
the ultimate technician, the greatest scientist. You looked at
false knowledge, ignorance, and science and opened up true
wisdom. You researched all forces and understood them. You
know which force can destroy another, which can control
another, and which can be used to create something else.
You have created all these magnets and forces. You are the
power, and with that power, You rule and control everything. There is no power that is similar to Your power, no
wisdom that is similar to Your wisdom, no qualities that are
similar to Your qualities, no words, actions, or conduct that
are similar to Your words, actions, and conduct, and no
compassion that is similar to Your compassion. There is
nothing that is similar to You. Other than You there is
nothing that all created lives can trust. They can believe only
in You. They must accept You. Those that accept Your
qualities have peace and tranquility. Those who act with
Your qualities, speech, words, and actions attain tranquility
and find heaven in their own lives. O Lord of the universes,
You are the One who created this condition. Everything
praises You—the earth, the sky, the sun, the moon, and all
created beings, earth lives, fire lives, water lives, air lives, and
ether lives. O Mighty One, there is no other Lord like You.
It is the One who has such power that we call the One God.

Other than You each energy, virus, force, or germ is
just a cell.[1] Different aspects arise from each cell and say, "I."
But every cell can be destroyed by another cell. Fire can burn

---

1. Throughout this talk Bawa Muhaiyaddeen says the word 'cell' in
English, but his use of this word is quite different from its standard
connotation. In his book *The Guidebook to the True Secret of the Heart, Vol. 1,*
two chapters are devoted to this subject. "God took one cell, a dot *(nuqat)*

the earth, water can destroy fire, air can move water, mountains and trees can block the currents of air. In this way, one thing controls another. The forces of the sun and moon can be subdued by clouds. The connection between the earth and the sky can be blocked by the clouds. When smoke and clouds are widespread, the earth cannot be seen from the sky nor can a person on land see the sky. This is how it is.

My love you, jeweled lights of my eye, my sisters, brothers, my daughters, sons, grandsons, and granddaughters. It is the same with our realization of the mystery of God. Just as the smoke and clouds can occlude the earth from seeing its connection to the sky and the sky from seeing its connection to the earth, the clouds of our mind and desire prevent us from seeing the connection between God and the hereafter (*ākhirah*) and our life in this world. These clouds prevent us from seeing the connection that exists between God and us. We fail to see our life-connection. These clouds are the four hundred trillion, ten thousand thoughts of our mind. These viruses, these cells, these clouds come and hide our connection to the future. They hide our connection to God. Religions, races, scriptures, philosophies, desires, attachments, blood ties, differences of colors, the many millions of thoughts, the thoughts of 'I' and 'you', property, livestock, wealth, desire for earth, women, and gold, and the thoughts of my house, my land, my wealth— these are the countless clouds brought about by the mind. Just as the clouds hide the sky from the earth, these clouds hide our connection to God and to the hereafter. They hide our clear connection to peace, and they hide the resplendence of life. By doing this, they prevent us from seeing the

---

from the *alif* (the Arabic letter for 'a' signifying the One Allah). He placed the eighteen thousand universes, the fifteen worlds, the appearances, hell, heaven, and everything within that one cell . . . . From that cell God has created everything else."

power of God and our connection to Him and the hereafter (*ākhirah*).

The mind causes all this to happen. If we transcend the mind, God will not be far away from our life. The two of us will be very close. One looks at the other, and both are in the same place. God and we are both in the same place. Within each of us, there is a place where God lives. He lives in a place of truth. He dwells in a place within us where we nurture our wisdom, words, actions, and conduct within His qualities. His qualities, actions, and three thousand gracious attributes are within a tiny piece of flesh. Without our realizing it, they exist in a specific region of our heart (*qalb*). God lives in that one place. The base desires rule over the rest of the body, but He rules over this divine kingdom. The rest of the body is ruled by cells, viruses, illusion (*māyā*), darkness, and fascinations. Each of these catch hold of and devour the other. As each one is being destroyed, it shouts, "My God." But the cell which is destroying it asks, "Who is God?" This is what happens when differences arise between two cells.

The clouds of the mind are the cause of these things. A person who transcends his mind will see the sky and the earth as one. He will know their connection. Just as the sky is seen when there are no clouds, the connection between God and man will be clearly seen when the mind is removed. When man can either transcend, control, or conquer the thoughts of mind and desire, the clouds of life that hide his vision will move away. When the clouds clear, the sky and the earth are clearly seen, are they not? Similarly, God, the hereafter, this world, and the truth in this world will be seen by man. Man *can* see this truth and understand it!

My love you, jeweled lights of my eye. Each child must reflect. There are certain ways in which God does things, and there is a reason why the things He does turn out right.

He puts everything in its appropriate place. God takes water and puts it back in water; water remains as water, and there is no difference. He takes fire, throws it back into fire, and there is no difference. He takes the eighty-four types of air and gases and places them back into the air, and there is no difference. He takes the earth, throws it back into the earth, it joins together, and there is no difference. He takes the earth and puts it into earth. He takes water and puts it into water. He takes the light of the sun and puts it back into light. He takes the cool colors of the moon and puts it into the moon. He takes something which glows in the dark and puts it into other things that glow in the dark. Luminous objects exist in the clouds, and as darkness descends they begin to glow. The moon has this ability also. When the light from the sky falls on the moon and clouds, they glow. That light is cool. The moon and sun both give light, but the sun's light is hot and causes heat and perspiration while the moon's light is cool.

If the moon is thrown into the sun, it will lose its power. When the sun emerges, the moon loses its power. When the sun dispels the darkness, the moon loses its power, because its power exists only in darkness. It is the same way when God gives wisdom to a man. As soon as the perfectly pure qualities of wisdom come into him, the world loses its power. Illusion (māyā) loses its power, the mind loses its power, attachments lose their power, and selfishness loses its power.

When God's qualities, God's actions, God's speech, and God's conduct come into us, the world will change into a powerless entity. All attachments will become powerless. The One Benevolence will show its compassion through its three thousand gracious attributes, and all lives will be seen as one's own life. All sorrow will be one's own, and all tiredness will be one's own. This is how the connection to truth begins, and in that state man does what God does. Truth is placed in the place of truth and is not destroyed. When God's words are placed in man's words, they are not destroyed; they are protected. Other forces cannot destroy that. When man adopts God's actions, and acts accordingly, they will not be destroyed. When God's vision, His thoughts, His focus, and the beautiful qualities of patience, contentment, surrender, and praise of God[2] are established in man, the qualities of all the cells are changed. In the face of these qualities, the four hundred trillion, ten thousand energies become powerless, and the clouds of the mind lose their power.

When God took water and placed it in water no differences could be seen. No differences could be seen when He put fire in fire, air in air, and earth in earth. When earth is stirred, earth mingles with the earth and becomes one. When clouds are beaten and stirred they join with other clouds and drift away. The mind can be made to leave in the same way. No matter what sins we may have gathered in our life, when we join truth with truth no differences will be seen. When wisdom is joined with wisdom there will be no differences. When God's qualities are joined with human qualities no differences will be seen. When we take on God's actions and act accordingly, there will be no differences. When we adopt God's conduct and act accordingly, there will be no differences. When we act with God's patience and contentment, when we act with surrender, praise of God, and His qualities, there will be no differences Then peace and tranquility enter our life, and our soul is liberated. The characteristics of God come within us, the light of God and the heart (qalb) of God come within us, and His resplen-

---

2. sabūr, shakūr, tawakkul, al-ḥamdu lillāh

dence of perfect purity comes within us. Then we realize
that we and God dwell in the same place. The clouds move
away and the darkness is destroyed and transformed. Mind
and desire are reduced and their thoughts are suppressed,
and peace, tranquility, and the kingdom of God can be
realized within us.

When this kingdom of God is known within us, we
realize the truth that God lives within us. We must understand this truth. This is the truth, but it can only be realized
in the place where no differences are seen. God joins each
thing to its appropriate section. He takes what is bad and
places it in evil, and He takes what is good and places it in
goodness. In this way, that which is bad will destroy other
things that are bad. Each of these bad cells will destroy the
other. But truth will not destroy anyone or anything. Therefore, truth has to be placed in truth, and good qualities have
to be placed in good qualities. These things will cause other
things to grow, whereas the bad things will only destroy.

God created the world, and it is through the world that
He will destroy the world. He created fire, and it is through
fire that He will destroy fire. He created air, and it is
through air that He will destroy air. He created water, and it
is through water that He will destroy water. He will destroy
the earth with the earth. He will ruin the sky with the sky.
Each cell can destroy another cell. But, truth will protect
truth and cause it to flourish. Similarly, each of our qualities
destroys another quality and causes us distress. It is our
thoughts that bring us difficulty. It is our intentions,
thoughts, and actions that torment us. Each of our thoughts
hurts us. Each of our attachments torments and tortures us.
Each selfish blood tie torments us over and over again and
cuts into us as if we were undergoing an operation.

Like this, it is our own thoughts that cause suffering,
difficulty, trouble, sorrow, and tears. It is our own thoughts

that cause our endless chatter and lack of peace. In our ignorance and lack of wisdom, we gather these things. These are the clouds that sever our connection to God. The connection between God's truth and us is a very close connection. God is closer to us than our own life, but our mind and desire hide that connection. Our thoughts, intentions, and attachments hide this connection. Once we push these things away, how easily the connection between God and us can be realized. The world disappears and the hereafter (ākhirah) opens up. Allah resplends, our heart (qalb) embraces Him, and there is bliss. There is peace!

We *can* attain peace and tranquility in our life. We must reflect on this. As long as we do not attain this state, it is our own evils that obstruct us. The cells and viruses that we ourselves cultivate are what bring us difficulty. These destructive cells will ruin our life. When truth is placed in truth, it grows and brings peace. God takes what is good and places it in that which is good, and there are no differences. He places what is bad with what is bad, and they continually destroy each other.

Religions, castes, and scriptures cause destruction. They are the cause of the destruction of the world. Each specific fire that each man keeps within him burns and destroys something else. The bombs that each man makes destroy other areas. Man's qualities destroy his own life as well as the lives of others. The five elements within him and the four hundred trillion, ten thousand qualities are the 'cells' that destroy the world. These cells, viruses, and germs are in man. They are like a magnetic force or an electrical current. When these qualities of 'I' and 'you' join with man, they are the cause of destruction. We must think about this. We must think about this.

My love you, my jeweled lights of my eye. Try to study within yourself. Understand within yourself and do this

research. The connection between God and us is a very close
one. It is so close, but the enormous mountain of the mind
keeps us from seeing it. Break down that mountain of arrogance, break down the 'I', and develop the mountain of
compassion. This mountain is soft like wax. It should be
developed in such a manner that it gives and bends with
melting love. These qualities of God must be developed. The
clouds, the storms, and the viruses of mind, desire, and
thoughts should be controlled and destroyed. The mountain
of arrogance should be broken down, and the desire that
says, "This is mine, this is mine," should be beaten and
removed. God's qualities of patience and contentment, trust
in God, giving all praise to God, and saying, "God is Great!"[3]
should be put there in their place. That station of peace
should be placed there. God's compassion and His qualities
should be placed there and protected. Then the resonance
and resplendence of the One of divine bliss, the Supreme
Treasure known as *Allāhu*, will be seen. The eight heavens of
this world and of the hereafter (*ākhirah*), the heavenly beings,
the prophets, the lights of God, the ones who explain, the
favorites of God, men of wisdom,[4] men of clarity, men with
unity and God's qualities will all be seen. As our wisdom
expands and keeps unfolding, this tiny place that the eye
cannot see becomes larger than the eighteen thousand
universes. It is a secret place of God. It is a place of peace, a
peaceful heaven. We can see this mysterious place, and if we
attain peace in this beautiful place, how blissful that will be.

My love you. Heaven and hell, good and bad do not
exist elsewhere. Our qualities alone are our heaven. It is what
we do, our actions, that constitutes our decreed destiny (*al-*

---

3. *sabūr, shakūr, tawakkul, al-hamdu lillāh,* and *Allāhu Akbar*
4. *nabīs, olis, qutbs, auliyā', gnānis*

qadā' wal-qadar). The pen is in our hands, and we write the
evidence that is considered for our final judgment. The final
decision is based on this writing. God looks at it and says,
"This is your destiny *(nasīb)*. We will make this your destiny."

In some situations, we try very hard to push things
away, and when it is beyond our limit we say, "That is our
destiny." We try all our remedies on someone who is sick,
and when they do not work we say, "That must be his destiny." In the same way, God also gives us the final judgment
saying, "This is his *nasīb*." He gave us everything. He gave us
all ninety-nine qualities and kept only one to Himself. He
says, "I gave man all My wealth, but man does not understand and comes to Me carrying the burdens of hell. Therefore, I will make that his destiny *(nasīb)*." So God says, "You
can return with the same things that you brought to Me."
God places His signature saying, "This is rightfully yours."

We create heaven and hell for ourselves. Whatever
aspect we develop becomes our own, and the resulting harm
or benefits are created by us. Do we take the section of hell
and try to destroy hell? No. We should push it aside and
move on. There is no need to destroy it, just move on. If a
dog comes to bite us, we just move on. We do not stop and
try to bite the dog in return. Similarly, when evil follows us,
we should tell it to go away and move on. We should not
spend time with it. It will shout for a while and then leave
Like this, the world will come swirling around us for a while,
but if we do not look back, it will go away. Sins will also
follow us for a while, but if we do not turn back, they will go
away. They will say, "This is not the place for us," and go
away. Many things will follow us for a while. If we look back
and smile broadly at them and become happy because of
them, then they will overcome us. But if we do not look at
them, they will go away saying, "This won't work. This man
will trample me. I cannot enter him."

Just as a prostitute dances and catches hold of a man, these viruses and this world catch hold of us. Like a prostitute, they decorate themselves with makeup, they dance, they act, and they catch hold of us. Each cell does this. All the four hundred trillion, ten thousand qualities do this in order to catch us. But if we do not look back at them, if we have faith, certitude, and determination in the One God and proceed along the path, they will not come near us. They will stay far away. They will follow us for a while and then leave us and go away.

Such things only come to catch hold of our mind and our qualities. If, the moment they try to latch onto our qualities, we throw them behind and move on, they will not affect us. They will promise us fame, gold, silver, women, palaces, and cities. They will clamor, "Look at this. Look at that. You can have it." But if you do not look behind, they will say, "We cannot do anything to this man," and go away.

The four hundred trillion, ten thousand thoughts come in this manner. If we drift toward them, laugh, and embrace them and feel happy, they will grab hold of us. But if we brush them away, they will leave. When a dog tries to bite us, we move on. We do not try to bite it back, because it will bite us. If we bend down it will bite us, if we stretch up or move it will bite us, if we pick up a stick or a stone it will bite us. Therefore, we must stand still and say, "O dog, why are you coming with me? Go away. I haven't harmed you. Just go away and do your work." Then the dog will move on and we can continue. We should do the same thing with each thing that comes to grab us. We should say, "Oh no, I am not coming with you. There is no need for you to follow me," and move on.

Why do the dogs of desire and the monkeys of the mind come and swarm around us? They come to catch hold of us. But there is no need to be afraid. If we look at them

without fear and say, "Go away monkey," it will leave. The
dog of desire snarls, growls, wags its tail, and walks around.
Just chase it away and it will lose its strength. The mind will
lose the strength of the 'I'; it will lose the strength of arrogance. Then it can be caught and tied up behind the kitchen.
The monkey of the mind and the dog of desire can be
caught and tied up, and we can do our work.

We have to reflect upon each of our thoughts. The four
hundred trillion, ten thousand spiritual energies try to kill,
devour, and destroy each other. Nothing good comes out of
this. One arises and tries to kill another, then another one
arises and tries to kill something else. This goes on and on.
Scriptures, religions, arrogance, karma, and differences of
colors that declare 'I' and 'you' are very similar to this. They
are all forces that destroy each other. But God's qualities and
actions, that truth, nourish everything and make everything
grow. Such is the power of God. Everything else is a cell or a
virus. They are like magnets that grab hold of things one by
one. These have magnetic energies, but God's qualities and
actions are a power and they have a connection to truth.
Everything else has a connection to these magnetic forces.

This energy is found in iron. A magnet can pull upon
the iron and separate it from the soil. Similarly, the magnet
of illusion, base desires, and cravings exists within man. If
this magnet comes near the mind, it exerts its pull upon the
mind. As long as the four hundred trillion, ten thousand
kinds of energies are present in the mind, they will be drawn
to the magnet of illusion and stick to it. This is the magnet
that pulls upon the desires and attachments of the senses.
Illusion pulls on the mind and separates us from God's
qualities.

This is the force of satan. Arrogance, *karma*, and illusion
(*māyā*); the three sexual energies which are the sons of
illusion (*tārahan, singhan,* and *sūran*); as well as desire, anger,

miserliness, infatuation, fanaticism, and envy; and the five heinous sins which are the use of intoxicants, lust, theft, murder, and falsehood—these seventeen forces or energies are the darkness within the mind of man. These magnets will pull on the four hundred trillion, ten thousand kinds of thoughts within man. Then they will draw man toward them saying, "Come, come, it is here, it is there," and show him different sights and scenes.

God's qualities, His truth, and His power are the only things that can put an end to these energies. These energies usually become caught in the net cast by the magnet. Only truth can change and transform these qualities. We should place truth among them. Then we can attain peace and tranquility, and we can see the kingdom of God within us. We will see God and the kingdom of God within us. We will see the Light known as Allah. We will see the good conduct, love, and affection which are His. We will see Him and know His state. We will see the value of God and the true value of man.

The outside form, the body, is not man. There is a man within him and that man is a resplendent soul. He has attained the resplendent light of the soul. Such a man is connected to God. Of the six kinds of lives, he is the man who is connected to God. Earth life dies when there is no earth. Fire life dies without fire. Water life dies without water. Air life dies without air. Ether life, which is the life influenced by the magnetic forces of illusion and its glitters, dies without ether. God life, the light, the life of man, the soul of God, will die without God. It lives in its connection with Him. These are the six kinds of lives. We must reflect on this.

Each one of these lives resides in a different place. If they do not have the connection to that particular place, they will die. There are the six kinds of lives, and we must analyze them with our six levels of consciousness. By doing this, if we can find out which life belongs to God, we will attain peace. If we ask who we are, we will find out that we have a connection to God, and that our souls are connected to His power and His ninety-nine attributes (*wilāyāt*) that control everything. All the creations have thirty-six characteristics (*tattwas*). Man has ninety-six. These, along with truth, absolute faith (*īmān*), and divine knowledge (*'ilm*) add up to ninety-nine. God is the hundredth power.

If man develops and acquires these ninety-nine within him, the hundredth one, the resplendence of God, the *Nūr*, will shine within him. Then he will have peace. That will be heaven and paradise. We must understand this. This is what is known as God. This is God. If we do not develop and acquire this state in the right way, then our life will be a hell that we ourselves have developed.

My children, it is we who prepare either heaven or hell for ourselves. Our destiny (*nasīb*) is written with our own hands, then handed over to God, and He gives the judgment. The good and evil (*khair* and *sharr*) are in Allah's responsibility; the essence and the manifestation (*dhāt* and *sifāt*) are developed by man. God has created us and given us the destiny of a created being. He has given us ninety-nine characteristics (*tattwas*) saying, "This is your destiny. Go accomplish what you have to with this and come back. If you gather good things, you will attain heaven, but if you gather what is evil, then you will attain hell. Whatever you bring back will be your final judgment. I will finalize that as your destiny. I am giving the decision of your destiny into your hand (*al-qadā' wal-qadar*). Go, finalize it, and come. Whatever conclusion you reach becomes your decreed destiny (*al-qadā' wal-qadar*)."

If we do not realize this and prepare hell for ourselves, then God will not give us heaven. God has *not* said, "Whatever I have given you is your destiny!" He will change your destiny according to your intention. Whenever you ask for forgiveness, instantly He will forgive you. As you repent and as your understanding of yourself increases, He will forgive you. As you intend Him more and more, He will grant you the benefits. If He had already written your destiny, He would not grant these things. He has given you the ability to repent (taubah), and He has given you forgiveness. Since He has given you both the faults and the remedy for it, He grants forgiveness when you ask for it.

Further, if God had already written your destiny, there would be no need to pray. Prayer has been reserved for you, so there is no such thing as predestination. For mankind, God has provided repentance, striving, and His forgiveness. Through these, you can gain victory. You should not say, "It is already written and there is nothing more to do." You must make an effort. He has given you the ninety-nine character-istics (tattwas) with which to strive. Ask and He will forgive. Intend Him and He will give. Ask; intend; He will give and forgive. If you knock, it will open. Ask and it shall be given. He will give.

Don't be foolish and worry about all the things you have heard people say. Use your wisdom and look deeply within. Allah says, "I will forgive. Ask for forgiveness, ask Me and I will give you what you ask." If He had already finished writing your destiny, then He would not grant this.

God waits until you are placed in the grave. He waits until the final Day of Judgment, and then He is the One who asks the questions. You are the one who brings the good and the bad. If He had already written the outcome, there would be no need for you to gather good or bad, and there would be no need for the One who had already written your des-tiny to stand in judgment. But because there is something for Him to judge, He is waiting to see what you bring. If He had already allotted hell to you, why would He have the two angels write an account of what you are doing? If there is something still to be written, then there is room for change and forgiveness. According to the good you do, there is heaven. According to the evil you do, there is hell. Use your wisdom.

Prophet Muhammad, the *Rasūlullāh* �, placed the Qur'an in the hands of his followers and said, "In order to understand this, go even unto China to learn divine knowledge (*'ilm*)." Within one word in the Qur'an, there are thousands of meanings. Don't hold on to just one meaning. Look within and there will be another meaning. Within that is another meaning, and within that is still another. As you uncover meaning after meaning, you will see Allah at the very end. When you go beyond all the messengers (*rasūls*) and look within, you will find Allah. The angels are also there. Go beyond them and look, go beyond everything and look, and then you will see heaven. Go beyond heaven, and Allah is there. Do not pray for heaven. Go beyond and look. Allah will be there.

We have to think about this. Each one of us must think about this and ask for forgiveness. Do not merely think, "Oh, I have done wrong." Instead, if you have done wrong, know that God is the Forbearant One who can forgive you. Ask Him and He will grant you forgiveness. Pray to Him. Worship Him. Allah is One who forgives. He is One who gives you what you ask. He is One who can change what has been written. Even though He is the One who gave it to you, He will change it for you. Even though He is the One who said it, He has the power to change it. Each one of you must think about this.

During our life, we must gather all that is beneficial. To do this, we must have absolute faith, certitude, and determination (*īmān*) in Almighty God (*Allāhu ta'ālā Nāyan*). We must

live our lives with this certitude; our words, our actions, and
our conduct must be as one. To receive His grace, we must
live and grow in this way, gathering the truth within our
heart (qalb). Our hearts must be God's treasure, and He must
be the life within our heart. If we can place that life, that
treasure, and His qualities within our heart and then bring
them into our actions, then that is the peace in our life and
that is heaven.

Precious jeweled lights of my eyes, every child must
reflect on this. In order to receive this benefit, try to live as
children with absolute faith, as children with wisdom, and as
children with certitude. May God help you toward this. May
the One of limitless grace, the One who is incomparable
love, grant you His grace.

O God, forgive us for whatever we have done earlier in
our ignorance, knowingly or unknowingly. May You forgive
us always for the wrongs we commit unknowingly and grant
us Your grace. Even though we have eyes, we are blind. Even
though we have a mouth, we are mute and unable to speak to
You. Even though we have a tongue, we are without the
tongue with which to talk with You. Even though we have
hands, we do not know how to receive Your goodness. Even
though we have the legs You gave us, we are unable to walk
to You. Even though You gave us the heart filled with the
plenitude of the light of Ahamad,[5] we do not know how to use
that heart to ask for forgiveness from You. Even with the
wisdom that You have given, we still do not know how to
speak to You and beseech You. We are fools. You created
and gave us the twenty-eight letters,[6] but we do not know

---

5. Ahamad is a Tamil variant of an Arabic word meaning the heart's
beauty visible on the face. See glossary.

6. The twenty-eight letters refer to the letters of the Arabic alphabet. Each section of the human form which will be questioned in the
grave is represented by one of these letters. When man purifies himself,
these letters take the form of light and appear as the eternal source of the
Qur'an (Ummul-Qur'ān) which was revealed to Muhammad ⊕.

how to speak to You or ask for forgiveness from You through each of those letters.

In the name of God, Most Merciful, Most Compassionate (*Bismillāhir-Rahmānir-Rahīm*). Whatever You begin and whatever You end is in Your hands. You are the Creator (*ar-Rabb*). You are the Compassionate One (*ar-Rahmān*). You are the Merciful One (*ar-Rahīm*). We cannot live without knowing You. You are the One who gives us our food and water. Because of that certainty, we have faith in You.

Please give us faith, certitude, and determination. O Creator, O Compassionate One, forgive us for all the faults we have done before this moment. Whatever faults my children and I have already committed, forgive us, and from now on, give us the clarity of wisdom and absolute faith. Give us good qualities and good actions and make us go on the good path. Give us an exalted life in this world, a life of living with You, a life of coming to You, a life in which You gather us unto You. May You make this a victory for us and grant us Your grace. O Allah, may You forgive all our sins. We committed them unknowingly in our ignorance. Forgive us. Forgive us. Please forgive us. So be it. So be it. So be it. O Ruler of the universes. *Āmīn. Āmīn. Āmīn. Yā Rabbal-'ālamīn.*

June 30, 1984

$$2$$

THE ANGEL OF DEATH AND THE
CREATION OF MAN

——————··⟨∞⟩··——————

In order to create the human race, God instructed that earth be taken from the four sides of *Karbalā'*,[1] which is the exact center of the eighteen thousand universes. This earth was to be made into one fistful and brought to Him and then placed at *Karbalā'*.

The Angel Jibrīl ☞ went to that central point to carry out Allah's instructions. But when Jibrīl ☞ tried to collect the handful of earth from the four directions, the earth said to him, "You are not meant to take earth from me, I swear on the name of Allah!" Next the Angel Mīkā'īl ☞, the ruler of water, and then Isrāfīl ☞, the ruler of air, were sent to accomplish this task. Each time, the earth gave the same reply, and they, too, could not fulfill the task.

Then God sent for the fourth angel, 'Izrā'īl ☞. 'Izrā'īl ☞ had four heads, four faces. One was black and very, very dark, one was a face of fire, one was like milk, and one was a beautiful face of light which was always focused on God. God told him, "Go down to that place and bring Me back the fistful of earth."

The earth gave 'Izrā'īl ☞ the same reply it had given to the angels Jibrīl, Mīkā'īl, and Isrāfīl, may the peace of God

———————————————

1. *Karbalā'* signifies the battlefield within the heart (*qalb*) of the human being. It is also a city in Iraq which has been a center of conflict throughout history.

27

be upon them. "I swear in the name of Allah, you are not meant to take earth from me."

But 'Izrā'īl ⊚ insisted, "This is the command of Allah! I am only doing what He told me to do. The very One upon whose name you are swearing is the One who told me to take this earth. Therefore, you and I have nothing to say to one another. You must talk to Him. I am just following His orders. If you do not want me to take this earth, speak to Him." So saying, 'Izrā'īl ⊚ collected the fistful of earth from the four directions and placed it at *Karbalā'*.

The earth collected from the four corners is illusion (*māyā*). It contains the elements of earth, fire, water, and air. God took these four elements, the four religions, the four steps, the four different kinds of prayers, and all the powers within them and compressed them into one handful of earth. In order to create man and to display the power of man, that fistful of earth was placed in the center point of the eighteen thousand universes called *Karbalā'*. What is this place? It is the human body. The central battlefield of the eighteen thousand universes is the inner heart of man (*qalb*). This is that one fistful of earth. Human beings have the five letters of earth, fire, water, air, and ether in their heart. They comprise the *A-L-H-M-D*.[2] Dogs have only one letter of Allah's power on the top of their head, and except for that one letter, their entire bodies are impure, hell.

If you try holding that heart in your hand, it will fit in the palm of your hand. All the fighting of the eighteen thousand universes occurs in this central place, the heart. Jinns, fairies, satans, the world, *māyā*, everything is here in this one fistful of earth. All the atom bombs are here. This is

2. *A-L-H-M-D*: The five letters, *alif, lām, mīm, hā', dāl* of the Arabic alphabet, which constitute the heart, become transformed in the heart of the true human being into *alhamd*, or *al-hamd*, the praise of Allah. See glossary.

the battlefield where every creation fights. This is the place
where destruction occurs, where profits are earned, where
creations live their lives and where they die. This is the place
where one kills others. It is the center of all lives, of all
creation and all mankind. Having created this, God placed
within it everything in its entirety—His secrets and His
grace as well as satan and ignorance, light and heaven as well
as darkness and hell. There is no fighting anywhere else.
This is where all the battles occur. Every life, every creation,
every man has to fight in this place.

The body of man, like that of a dog, grows in desire.
Just as a dog grows by eating dirt and feces, the human body
also grows from disgusting things. A snake charmer, who was
a wise man (*munivar*), once sang this song:

> Taking the earth from the pit of dirt,
> Mixing it with the blood in the womb,
> This body made by the Master Potter
> Will be of less use than a piece of a broken pot.
> So dance on, O snake,
> Play on, O snake,
> As the ornament of Lord Shiva,
> Dance on, O snake!
> The wise man was singing to the mind, to the senses,
> What was all this created from?
> It originated from the pit of dirt, the place of birth,
>   the womb,
> This place is dirty,
> The menses and urine pass through it.
> Into that bag of the uterus, He puts this earth,
> Mixes it with the blood,
> And He makes the embryo.
> This body made by the Master Potter
> Will be of less use than a piece of a broken pot.
> So dance on, O snake.

That form created by foul liquid joining with the blood in the uterus, that body, the toy, which was made by the Master Potter, God, is of less use than a piece of a broken clay pot. A broken piece of pot can at least be used for something, like heating and mixing herbal medicines, but this body does not even have that much use. "So dance on, O snake! This body is of no use." This is what the wise man once sang.

Everything is useless except for this central place where God has placed all His powers, grace, wealth, justice, and truth. But ghosts, demons, jinns, satans, illusion (māyā), smells, desires, darkness, and lights also come to that place. Dogs, foxes, cats, mice, elephants, lions, tigers, rhinoceroses, bears, and other animals also come there. That is the battle-field. And when they come, you have to combat them with wisdom and grace, with faith, certitude, and determination (īmān). With God, stand as God, and fight against them.

God has placed all the eighteen thousand universes as well as His secrets and mysteries within that central place. Having created it from that fistful of earth and having given it great value, God made it into His treasury. On one side there is the secret and on the other side is the treasury. If you examine it, you will discover that it is an endless secret, and if you go to take from it, it is a limitless treasury of God, a wealth beyond wealth. It is from this that God created man. The body that the Master Potter created is of less use than a broken piece of a pot, but that central place is a great secret. One will destroy you and the other will nourish you.

When 'Izrā'īl ⊕ brought this fistful of earth, God told him, "You managed to bring the earth which the other three angels were unable to bring. Therefore, I am going to bestow an honor upon you, and you must accept it. Henceforth, you will have the job of the Angel of Death. What you brought Me, I will decorate and send back to the world. I will place all of My secrets, My powers, and the eighteen thousand universes within it. I will also place within it all aspects of creation and all its beauty. Within that secret, within the power of the earth, I am going to place My resplendent light (*Nūr*), My rays, the rays of My power, the soul. This is My entrusted treasure which I am going to give everyone. It is the soul. I am going to place it within that fistful of earth and send it to the world. You will have to go there, locate this treasury, and look into its accounts, its nature, and its duration, and then you will have to bring My entrusted treasure back to Me. You brought Me the earth originally, and in order to bring My treasure back to Me, I am sending you into this world once again. Return the earth to the earth, and bring back to Me what belongs to Me. I will name you 'Izrā'īl, Yaman, the Angel of Death."

"Oh, God!" 'Izrā'īl ☜ cried out, "I do not want this job. Everyone will scold me. I do not want this job."

"Why will they scold you?" God asked.

"Because I will have to leave the child behind and take the mother, I will have to leave the mother and take the child, I will have to leave the wife and take the husband, and I will have to leave the older brother and take the younger brother. If I follow Your instructions, everyone will curse me. They will say, 'Yaman is a terrible person, why doesn't he die? Doesn't he have the eyes to see?' Everyone in the world will curse me. I will be subject to sin and blemish. Both good people and bad people will consider me as one who does evil. I will be the cause of their grief. Oh God, I do not want this job. Please give it to someone else."

Then God replied, "O 'Izrā'īl, I know this. But no one will blame you. Listen to what I say. Within all the beings that I created, I have placed 4,448 illnesses. Every section, every point has been placed within them according to their destiny. I have written their accounts and placed them within them. Everything is within man. I am sending the disease that will kill him along with him. He himself has the medicine that can kill him, and he himself has the medicine that can save him. The remedy to escape will also be within him. He will know all this. This treasury will exist within every being that I create. I have kept the nourishment, his food (*rizq*) and water for him. I am the One who provides all of this. You should go there, look at his heart, and understand what he has within there. You should see what his illness is and what will be the cause of his death. Whatever he has sought is what will cause his death.

"If a snake ought to bite him, then you will take the form of a snake. If a bull ought to butt him, then you will take the form of a bull. If a mountain ought to fall on his head, then you will take the form of a mountain. If he is to die from a fever, then you will take the form of a fever. If he is to die due to blood pressure, then you have to take the form of blood pressure. You have to take whatever form is necessary. If he is to die by asphyxiation from gas, then you will take the form of gas. If he is to die by being hit by a falling rock, then you will take the form of a rock. This is only a dream. To the body these events will be like a dream. Whatever has been written at the time of creation (*awwal*), regarding the way in which he should die, along with whatever he has sought in the world, those are what will cause his death.

"No one will say that 'Izrā'īl ☺ caused his death. Instead they will say that he died from a fever, an accident, an avalanche, a motor accident, or by falling from a tree or being hit by a rock; or he died from falling into a deep pit, or from a fractured leg or arm or some other injury. This is what they will say. The blame will not be placed on you. Do not worry about this. No one will obstruct or oppose you in your work. You will continue to do this job until *Qiyāmah*, the Day of Reckoning, and finally I will summon you back. If you should waver from justice or stray from My commands in the way you treat My creations, I will deal with that in the end. You are the Angel of Death. After you have brought back the lives of My creations, I will take your life through your own agency. It is easy to take the lives of others, but think about how difficult it will be to bring your own life back to Me. That is the subtlest of mysteries." So spoke God to 'Izrā'īl (☞).

We were created in this manner. The cause of our death is created by no one other than ourselves. We seek it out through our own actions. We are the ones who seek hell and we are the ones who seek heaven. It is we who seek the earth, the light, the falsehood, ignorance, or illusion (*māyā*). None of this is God's fault. Whatever we cultivate will either save us or lead to our death. This plan has been placed within us. If we do not understand this, then the very things we seek in our life will cause our death.

If a person raises a snake by giving it milk, then one day, no matter how well he raised it, that snake will cause his death. If a person becomes absorbed in his passion for riding horses, then one day he will fall off the horse and die. If a person enjoys his life riding on a bull, then he will die from being butted by that same bull. If a person is constantly drinking alcohol, then alcohol will cause his death one day. A snake charmer who makes a snake dance now will one day die from that snake. A man who makes an elephant do work will be killed by that elephant. A person who worships demons will be killed by those demons. A person who worships satan will die by satan. A person who uses *mantras* to perform magic will die because of his *mantras*. Whatever a person uses, whatever a person does, whatever form he creates, that will be the cause of his destruction and his death.

All these things that we hold on to will change. God is the only thing that does not change and cannot be destroyed. That Treasure will harm no one. It bestows everything upon others, never asking anything for itself. It has no shadow, no form, no wife, no birth, no darkness, no torpor, no anger, no thirst, no jealousy, no vengeance, no 'I' and 'you'. That Treasure has no arrogance, hastiness, or differences of 'mine' and 'yours'. It does not earn anything for itself. It is One that never acts against its conscience. It is a treasury of justice, the One that inquires and dispenses justice. That is the God of perfection. It only gives and never receives.

Everything else that a person creates or raises will behave differently. If he brings up a lion, he will have to feed it with flesh or it will devour him some day. If a person raises an elephant, he will have to feed it with fruits, otherwise it will trample him some day. If a person raises a tiger, he has to feed it with flesh. If he does not feed it, one day it will kill him. If a person raises a snake, he has to feed it with eggs, milk, or rats and still it will kill him. If a person raises a cat, he has to feed it with rats, dried fish, or meat, but the person's death can be caused by either the cat's breath, or its hair, or its saliva. His illness could develop from that. Similarly, if a person worships satan, offering him milk and fruits and performing ritual worship (pūjās), that very same satan will come and kill him one day.

Whatever a person does, that same thing will cause his death. It is something that we raise ourselves, and if we try to oppose it, there will be a huge battle. If we seek to understand the truth, there will be a fight. God is One, but the world is 'many'. God is One Power, but there are many demons. God is One, but the seeds of illusion (māyā) are many. The demons, ghosts, devils, and satans are very selfish and have the arrogance of the 'I'. They have the power of

killing others. What they want to do is to somehow catch
and devour all of God's creations. They like to suck blood,
bodily secretions, and even the foul-smelling secretions from
a corpse. They will also suck the blood out of a living being.
Some demons will suck the semen out from a human being.
Other demons are attracted to the smell of the blood and
saliva and they take that. There are demons like this.

If you were to raise a dog, for instance, no matter what
type of food you may give it, when you touch it or carry it,
what will it do? It will vigorously lick your mouth. Why does
it place its tongue inside your mouth instead of licking you
somewhere else? Because your saliva has germs in it and
these germs have a foul smell, the smell of blood. The saliva
also has the essence of all the food that you have eaten.
These odors are appealing to the sensitive nose of a dog. As
soon as the dog smells your mouth, it tries to lick it and taste
your saliva.

Similarly, whatever possessions of satan you carry in
your mind, if you carry the bloody odors of 'mine' and
yours', my wealth and your wealth, 'I' and 'you', my house
and your house, my race and your race, if your mind carries
anything that is created out of the blood, the attachments, or
the secretions, satan will perceive that smell. Satan will see
those intentions, those qualities, and those blood ties. He
will see the world (dunya) and those desires. When he sees
these things, he will say, "These are my possessions," and he
will come and lick you vigorously. Just as the dog licks your
mouth when it smells the odor, if satan detects that smell in
you, he will come. He will come and lick if you have any
anger, sin, falsehood, vengeance, selfishness, the thoughts of
'mine' and 'yours', my child and your child, or the attachments of blood ties. Even if we leave the world, if we had
these things in our mind, satan will come and lick us. This is
the explanation that we must understand.

God is not like this. He is in everything. God knows who His child is, but it is only when the child realizes himself and comes forward that God will call him the 'son of God'. God will bestow His title on him. But if the child does not realize himself, God will feel no sorrow. He has no grief. This is the point. It is to do this work that God created the Angel of Death.[3] We are the ones who invite the Angel of Death. We are the ones who create the illnesses through which we die and it is we who create the agreement of our destiny. But we must try to see the section that can cut through this. We must try to understand what needs to be understood in order to die before death. There is a sign for 'Izrā'īl ☺ to come. This sign or allotted agreement belongs to earth, fire, water, air, and ether. This is the world. The mind, birth, arrogance, karma, illusion (*māyā*), the desires and visions of the mind constitute our world. If any of these things are with us, then 'Izrā'īl ☺ comes. But if the mind dies then desire will die, if desire dies then the visions of pleasure will die, if those visions die then illusion will die, if illusion dies then karma will die, if karma dies then the world dies, and if the world dies then the agreement is nullified. There will be no desire, blood ties, differences, or anger. Everything we had before will have left. Nothing will remain. Then there is no death for us. When we are in that state, the Angel of Death will not come. Then there is only light.

This is the way to die before death. This is the section that we have come here to understand. We must realize this Power.

'Izrā'īl ☺ lives between the gallbladder and the liver.

----

3. At this point in the original talk, Bawa Muhaiyaddeen told the long story "Sandakumaran meets the Angel of Death" which was previously published in its entirety in Chapter Four of the epic tale *Maya Veeram or The Forces of Illusion*.

Satan lives in the bile. Mīkā'īl ⓔ lives in the spleen. Isrāfīl ⓔ is in the lungs. The one who lives in the *Bismin kāi* [4] is Jibrīl ⓔ; the one on the right side is the *Nūr*, or Muhammad ⓔ; and the One who is within the heart *(qalb)* is the Merciful One *(Rahmān)*, the Truth *(Haqq)*, Allah. Munkar and Nakīr ⓔ ask the questions in the grave. Raqīb and 'Atīd ⓔ, the two angels who write down the account of good and bad, are on the shoulders. The angel on the left shoulder records the bad and the angel on the right records the good. God has placed those witnesses right here with us. Therefore, we cannot escape. Every single breath of ours is recorded. We do not need to take a witness along with us when we die. Everything has been recorded already, and that tape will be played there.

It is similar to the radar that takes a picture of every car that is speeding. When the case is taken to court, there can be no lies or arguments. It will not help to take a lawyer or intermediary to plead on your behalf. Everything has been recorded on film. They will just take away your license or issue a fine. That will be the judgment.

In the same way, everything you do here is recorded. You cannot lie about it when you go there. The pictures and the questioning will be on record. That is how it is. Everything has been placed within us. We have to understand this.

July 21, 1973

---

4. There is a piece of flesh, a node on the right surface of the heart, next to the lung, called the *Bismin kāi*. The *Bismin kāi* is the place in the body where faith is strengthened and where the *dhikr*, the remembrance of God, is established. See glossary.

3

THE CHILDREN OF ADAM ☺

————❦————

May God protect us from satan, the rejected one.
(A'udhu billāhi minash-shaitānir-rajīm.) In the name of
God, the Most Merciful, Most Compassionate. (Bismillāhir-
Rahmānir-Rahīm.) May all praise and praising be to Allah, the
One who is limitless grace and incomparable love, the One
who gives us of His infinite wealth of grace. May He bestow
His beneficence and His grace upon us. Āmīn.

He is the One who is the most worthy. With Your
grace and beneficence, may You protect us. We need Your
help throughout our life. Even in death we need Your help.
We need Your help for eternal life (hayāt). We need Your
help in the hereafter (ākhirah), and we need Your help in this
world (dunyā). You are the Father for our lives, the Father
who protects us, the Father who sustains us, the Father who
creates us and protects us. You are the One who gives us
Your grace, the One who is the infinite wealth. You create
the light of our soul with such beauty and You protect us.
We need Your help everywhere. May You protect us, O
God. Āmīn. Āmīn.

My love you, my brothers and sisters, my daughters and
sons, my grandsons and granddaughters. My love you. The
creations of God are of many different kinds. We are the
children of Adam ☺. We are all children of one father and
mother. Adam ☺ was created by God out of clay, without a
father and mother. Then God took one rib from Adam ☺
and created Hawwā' (Eve) ☺. Thus, He also created Hawwā' ☺
without a father. And in the same way, God created Jesus ☺

39

without a father, without semen. So Adam, Hawwā', and Jesus (may the peace of God be upon them all), these three beings were created without semen.

The children of Adam ☺, all who have faith in God and who trust in God are from the family of Abraham ☺, while those who have lost their faith belong to satan and are from the family of satan. They have changed, and their lives have become lost. All who have faith and who have patience (sabūr) belong to the tribe of Abraham ☺, and it is this state which makes them followers of Muhammad ☺. They are the same tribe, the same group, with the same truth, all brothers and sisters in one family.

It is unity that creates one family, one tribe. There are three aspects to that unity. We all are in one family with the same father and mother, Adam and Eve ☺. We all have one ancestry, the tribe of Abraham ☺. And we all are the followers of Muhammad ☺; that is, we love, trust, and believe in the One God.

Twenty-five prophets have been mentioned in the Qur'an. God gave the same teaching to each of these prophets, one after the other. These twenty-five were amongst 124,000 prophets that God sent down. They could speak with God. Allah spoke to them from within. Other times He spoke to them through Gabriel ☺, with Gabriel ☺ as the witness. At other times, He spoke from within them, as grace—to the wise men, to the saints of God, the prophets, the explainers of wisdom, the lights, the learned ones and scholars, the ancient astrologers, and many others.[1] We have to reflect upon these things.

Our beauty is within us, our search is within us, and our paradise is within us. Heaven is within us. Each person's

---

1. *gnānis, auliyā', ambiyā', qutbs, olis, 'ālims, 'ulamā', nujumis*

search, his paradise, his beauty, his light, his purity, and his radiance reside within himself—not elsewhere or within others.

Thus, whatever we seek will emerge from within ourselves. It will emerge from our hearts. It will be revealed from our faces. It will manifest in the sounds we make and in our actions. It will show itself in our qualities and in our speech. It will be evident in our conduct. That is how God's beauty is revealed—His qualities can be seen as they emerge from His children.

God is the One who knows the state of each child. If you see a mother at the riverside, you do not have to go to the house to see what the child is like, because the mother's beauty and qualities will be reflected in the child. If the mother's qualities are bad, the child will have bad qualities. If the mother is terrible, the child will be terrible. On the other hand, if the mother is beautiful both in looks and in qualities, the child will be also.

Our Father, God, is perfect purity, the most Beautiful One, the Solitary One, *ill-Allāh* who is alone. He is the One who rules so many millions and millions of souls and creations, the 8,400,000 different kinds of lives, things that move and things that do not move, things that speak and things that do not speak, things that crawl and things that do not crawl, every current and every energy. He is the cause for the rocks to grow. He is the cause that makes the seeds grow. He is the cause that makes the embryos grow and the atoms grow. If not for Him not even an atom would move.

The qualities, actions, and beauty of such a Creator, such an Almighty One, are passed on to us, because He is our Father and our Mother. God is the Pure One, the Beautiful One, the One who is alone, *Allāhu*, our Father. When His qualities, His actions, and His conduct become ours, then

He becomes our Mother and Father. Who was Adam's ☾
Mother and Father? God. He created Adam ☾. In the same
way, when we become eternal beings, God becomes our
Mother and Father. When we are transformed to the state of
eternal life, God is our Mother and Father. In that state, we
can know His beauty, His light, His sound, and His qualities, His three thousand gracious qualities and His ninety-
nine attributes (wilāyāt).

He does not have the quality of differences. His quali-
ties are those of protecting, sustaining, and giving food, the
quality of embracing on the inside and the outside. He is the
Emperor. He is the Protector of all the worlds. He is the
Almighty One. He is the Great Father, Yahweh. Everything is
within Him and He is within everything. Yā Rabbal-'ālamīn,
O Ruler of the universes. Yā Rahmān, the Most Merciful, Yā
Allāh! The One who never diminishes as you go on taking
from Him. When His qualities and His beauty come to us,
His sound will come to us. He is the Mother of the soul.
When that beauty and those qualities come to us, He will
embrace us as His children. What other approval do we
need?

All the animals know God's fragrance, that fragrance.
When they perceive that fragrance, all lives worship it. The
cows, goats, chickens, and storks, all the animals bow down
to it. To the satans, jinns, demons, and ghosts it is a fierce
fire. It burns them and they run away. But to all other lives it
is a beautiful fragrance. God's light is the fragrance. Evil runs
away from it, and goodness embraces it. All that is good will
come and join God. All that is evil will be burned. This is the
great power of God's qualities.

When we receive this beauty, it is visible in our actions.
No other proof is needed; the beauty is evident within us. It
is apparent in every child. The beauty of the Father shines
from the children. The beauty of the Mother is there. The

beauty of the eternal Father is there. His sound is there. His qualities come to them. His patience comes to them. The Father's exaltedness is seen in them, and because of this they receive so much respect. They become younger. They do not look like old men or old women. Their faces are clear of wrinkles and shimmer and shine with the beauty of flowing milk. Such is the beauty and greatness of the sound, speech, actions, and conduct of our Father. And when we have that beauty, we will know ourselves. We will know the state where all lives bow down in reverence. Whatever we say will be respected. Everything that comes to our tongues will be sweet. It will be very tasty to the ones with wisdom. But those who have no wisdom will find it a little bitter.

Many different kinds of concoctions and herbs and medicines are given to promote strength and vigor and to cure the illnesses of the body. In the same way, God's words, the ocean of 'ilm, of divine knowledge, are given for the freedom, the beauty, and the resplendence of the soul. The taste of that 'ilm is given in so many different ways, through speech, through the breath, and through actions. It nourishes the cage of the soul. It makes the soul young and beautiful and adorns the house in which the soul dwells. That beauty comes from that 'ilm and is seen in one's qualities and actions. We can see the proof of this in each child. We can see it in ourselves and in the other children around us.

My love you, my children. You will realize the purity of the words in yourself and see the great value in yourself. That greatness and beauty, that form, and those qualities will be seen in you, yourself. When all the words of your Father come within you and shine, that beauty of your Father's words, actions, and conduct will come also into you. The qualities of patience, contentment, surrender to God, and giving all praise to God (sabūr, shakūr, tawakkul 'alallāh, al-hamdu lillāh) will enter within you.

Allāhu Akbar, God is Great. He is the Father to all of us. Is He not the One who is limitless grace? He gives grace. He is the One who gives His beneficence. He gives to all lives. For goodness He gives eight heavens, and for evil He opens the seven hells. Where each person will go is determined by what he sought in life.

When we die, nothing will go with us except the good and the evil we have done. Not our race. Not our religion. Not our caste. There will be no inquiry as to what race we are, what religion we are, or what caste we are. Only one thing will be evident, whether we are male or female. That is all.

When death comes, our form will change. It will be made of our qualities. If our qualities in the world were like those of a pig, we will take the form of a pig. If we had the qualities of a donkey, we will take the form, the face, of a donkey. If we lived with the qualities of a horse, a snake, or a dog while we were in this human body, then we will assume that form there. The form that we created through our qualities in this world is the form we are going to take after our bodies are claimed by the earth. It is of those forms that the questions will be asked. These forms of dogs, lions, tigers, and others have tongues hanging out that are one-and-a-half feet long. When the word *"Kun!* (Be!) Arise!" comes, it is *these* corpses that are raised up. These are the forms you will see when they are raised up. The form each one takes will be according to the benefit each one sought, the property each one gathered, the capital each one earned, and the intentions each one had.

When the day of inquiry comes, they do not ask about your caste. The questions that are asked will be, "Who is your *Rabb* (Lord)? What is your tribe? To whose family do you belong?"

"I am a child of Adam ⊛. I am of the good ones, the

family of Abraham ☮, and I am a follower of Muhammad ☮."
There are six questions that will be asked.

As soon as you see the two angels, Munkar and Nakīr ☮,
give them *salāms* with love, saying, "Peace be with you. (*As-
salāmu 'alaikum.*) Welcome." Their flaming, fiery faces and
fiery eyes will change and become subdued.[2] Then one by
one the questions will be asked, and you must answer. There
will be no place for race, for this religion or that religion.
The questions that are asked will be about the One who
created us and about the one who was created, Adam, *insān*,
mankind. This is what will be asked, and we have to answer
these questions. We cannot say we belong to this group or
that group.

For everyone, God has placed in heaven Adam, Noah,
Abraham, Ishmael, Moses, David, Jesus (may the peace of
God be upon them all), and finally Muhammad *Mustafar-
Rasūl* ☮, the chosen Messenger. God has sent Idris, Isaac,
Joseph, Jonah, Job, Jacob, Sālihu, and Solomon (may the
peace of God be upon them all). All were sent by the One
God, and that One God gave them their stations. We are all
one tribe—human beings. We may be black or white or
yellow or brown, but we are all one race—human.

What people do in the East, they also do in the West.
They kiss the same way, they embrace the same way, they
bear children the same way. They do exactly the same
things. They eat the same way, although they may have
different kinds of food, depending upon what is available in
their country. The way a child wails there, a child wails here.
"Amo, oh moh! Mow, mee!" A child makes the same sounds
whether in the East or West. There, children sleep, wake up,

---

2. A further description of these angels and what transpires in the
grave was given by M. R. Bawa Muhaiyaddeen on June 6, 1984 and
published in the pamphlet "The Questioning in the Grave."

and cry. Here too. No matter what race they belong to, no matter what religion they belong to, they cry in the same way. Do they say different things? No. When they start to talk, they make the same sounds. They sit up the same way. They sway and fall over. They crawl on all fours. This is the human race.

What the children come with is the original teaching. What we teach them after that in the schools and in other places is the temporary teachings of differences between races and religions. Before they were all one. If they were asked, "Who is your God? What is your tribe, your family?" they would have given these same answers, "We are the children of Adam ⊛, we are of the family of Abraham ⊛, and we are the followers of Muhammad ⊛." These are the three answers that will be given. All the prophets are included in this. These are the answers that come when Munkar and Nakīr ⊛ ask the questions.

When we are raised up, we will rise up in the form that we have assumed through our qualities. They will say, "Write!"

And we will say, "We have no pen, no ink."

Then they will say, "Touch your finger to your saliva."

"But I have no paper to write on."

"Write on your burial shroud. Touch and write. You have the ink. Write down on your shroud all that you have done." When you are raised up tomorrow, you will have to go in the form that you have assumed, and then the judgment will come.

O God please protect us. Save us from the suffering in the grave. Save us from the suffering in life. Save us from the suffering caused by our evil qualities. Save us from the qualities of religious and racial prejudice. Save us from the battlefield of "I am different. You are different." Save us from the circumstances that surround these battles and murders, the situations where people drink our blood and where one being kills and eats the other.

Allah! Protect us and take us on the straight path. Please give us Your grace to always walk freely on Your path. Grant us liberation, divine wisdom (*gnānam*), Your grace, exaltedness, light, and paradise in life. Grant us the heaven that is Your wealth (*daulat*). May You give these to us, O God. Please forgive us our sins, all the sins that we committed before, without knowing, when we were without wisdom. This does not mean that we have attained wisdom. You are the One of wisdom. You are the One of beauty. You are the One who has love and good qualities. You are the One of compassion and patience. You are the One who has equality and tolerance. You are the One with unity and the highest ideals. You are the One who brings us all together as one, and You are the One who rules over all as one. You are the Lord, the King of all kings, the Father of all lives. You are the Leader who protects all lives, the One who is everywhere, *ill-Allāh*. You are the One who is as You are at all times, the One who is alone, the One who is One. You are the Father to the millions of lives, the Eternal Father, the Redeemer of all the worlds, the Eternal Treasure of bliss who exists everywhere as the Lone One, the Leader to all lives that exist as the many.

We are Your slaves. May You protect us, O God. May You accept us, O God. May You protect us, O God. O being of eternal bliss, may You forgive all our mistakes. Please forgive us all our faults, O God. Even though we cannot see You, O God, we have trust in our heart (*qalb*). Even though we do not know You, our *qalb* trusts You with certitude. It is trying to know You. Even though we do not know how to recite, even though we do not know anything, we believe in You. With our foolish wisdom, we believe in You.

May You protect us. Save us who do not know anything. Please forgive us for all the faults we have committed. We do not have divine knowledge (*'ilm*). We have not learned anything. We do not know how to speak. We do not know how to pray. We do not know how to perform service to God (*'ibādat*) or the remembrance of God (*dhikr*). We are doing all this without knowing how. We do not know how to do it.

Prayer done without knowing how to pray,
Prayer done without knowing any method,
The prayer we perform in this world,
We pray without understanding prayer
   and worship.
Almighty God, we perform prayer without
   knowing anything.
I do not understand prayer,
I do not know about formal prayer (toluhai).
I have not learned how to recite or read,
I have not learned how to recite or read.
We are agitating in suspense, living here like corpses,
And we scream and wail without knowing divine
   knowledge ('ilm).

I am suffering, not comprehending the differences of
   race and religion.
Perfectly pure Almighty God,
I believe that You are One.
I am perplexed, not understanding the divisions of race
   and religion,

I believe that my Chieftain, God, is One,

And I praise You as the primal, all-pervasive
   Effulgence.

I am Your slave, Your slave, O God who rules us and
   bestows grace,

I am Your slave, Your slave, O God who rules us and
   bestows grace.

Show us how to pray,

Teach us how to recite and read,

Show us the way to pray and perform service to
   You ('ibādat).

O God, open and reveal the truth to me and
   my children,

O God, show the way to me and my children,

O God, show the way to me and my children,

Show us the purity of the heart.

With Your grace bestow the certitude and absolute
   faith (īmān)

With which to worship Your love,

To worship that one Treasure in unity,

To live together always as one race,

To embrace all lives with love as one.

Feed us Your grace to embrace with faith
   and worship

The light of grace, the divine luminous light,

The radiance of the pearl of gnānam,

The light of wisdom, the divine luminous light,
The light of the pearl of gnānam, as God.
O primal omnipresent Effulgence,
May You embrace us and feed us with
      Your grace,
May You forgive all the faults that we have
      committed unknowingly.
You are the God who rules all three worlds,
May You embrace us.
We are sinners known to no one,
Embrace and rule us, O God, Allāhu.
Feed us with Your compassion,
Open Your eye and look at us.

Earth, illusion (māyā), and thoughts come
And entice us and make us lose our honor.
All the discriminations and differences of race
      and religion
Come and disturb and confuse us.
Discriminations of race and religion come
      and crush us,
Every second they torment us.
What can we do?
What can we do, O God?
They are tormenting us, what can we do, O my God?

Just as You escaped from all these,

May You help us escape from these, O Merciful One.
Protect us, O God,
Protect and save us, O God,
O God who is beyond all imagination,
Protect us, O God,
Look and bestow Your grace on us, O God.
The Treasure of eternal bliss, O Ruler,
Qādir, the Powerful One, Dastagīr, the Lord,
The Eye, the Gem, our Causal Light,
The Perfect Completeness, God, Allāhu,
May You dispel the sorrows of these poor ones
And protect all of us.
May You dispel the sorrows of these sinners
And protect all of us, O God.
Look at us all, save us all,
O Treasure of eternal bliss.

O great Father, O God,
O King, Rabbil-'ālamīn, Lord of all
   the universes,
O Rahmān, O Merciful One,
We need Your beneficence.
Be the Life within our lives.
Open the qalb of truth,
Feed it the honey of grace.
Cause the blissful 'ilm, wisdom, clarity, and īmān to
   flourish and grow.

You are the fruit of wisdom (gnānam) that makes
    them grow.
I must eat that fruit of wisdom,
The fruit of gnānam and the fruit of grace
And relish the taste.

Please help me and my children, O God of bliss,
O God, Yā Rabbal-'ālamīn,
O Lord of all the universes.
Āmīn.
As-salāmu 'alaikum.
May the peace of God
    be with you.

                                    June 3, 1984

4

The Pathway to Paradise

———————— ⦿ ————————

May God protect us from satan, the rejected one. (*A'ūdhu billāhi minash-shaitanir-rajīm.*) In the name of God, Most Merciful, Most Compassionate. (*Bismillāhir-Rahmānir-Rahīm.*) I testify that there is no god except the One God, that He is One without associates, and I testify that Muhammad is His servant and His Messenger. (*Ash-hadu al-lā ilāha ill-Allāh wahdahu lā sharīka lah, wa ash-hadu anna Muhammadan 'abduhu wa rasūluh.*)

May Allah, the Lord of the universes (*Rabbul-'ālamīn*), embrace our whole family within His beauty. May He take us all to that one place, to paradise. O Allah, please forgive the faults my children may yet commit, and please forgive the faults they may have already committed, both knowingly and unknowingly. Forgive all of them, O Allah. Please take all of my children to Your station. My children are Your children, O Allah. Give them a place in heaven, give them a beautiful place within Your good grace and give them Your blessing. There is none other than You, O Lord. You are One. Please take my children to Your kingdom.

You have no equal, no parallel. You are the undiminishing wealth, the complete wealth, O Allah. You are the One God to all of the prophets and to all of us. Take all of my children unto You. So be it, O Ruler of the universes. So be it. (*Āmīn, Yā Rabbal-'ālamīn. Āmīn.*)

In the name of God, Most Merciful, Most Compassionate. (*Bismillāhir-Rahmānir-Rahīm.*) What is known as God is One and what is known as man (*insān*) is also one—one community, One God. O Allah, may this one community accept You as the One Leader. You alone are the Chieftain for mankind (insān), as well as the Supreme Being for all lives in the world. Our life, the life of man, is to accept You as the One Leader. Through Your prophets, You made us accept You. You made us accept the prophets and their followers. You have also told us to accept the angels, the heavenly beings, and the illumined beings.

The angels and the archangels that we have accepted are a part of us. The angels Jibrīl ☺, Mīkā'īl ☺, Isrāfīl ☺, 'Izrā'īl ☺, Rūqā'īl ☺, Munkar and Nakīr ☺, Raqīb and 'Atīd ☺, and Ridwān and Mālik ☺ continually ask for good on our behalf. We have to accept these angels.

O Allāhu, because You have directed us to accept You, Your angels, Your archangels, and all aspects of You, we accept them and recite this kalimah (affirmation of faith). We accept this kalimah, Your prophets, You, and everything You told us to accept. This is our intention. Tomorrow, on the day of questioning (qiyāmah), You will question us, and we must be ready to answer those questions.

Precious children, jeweled lights of my eyes, God is limitless grace and incomparable love. He is the bestower of the undiminishing wealth of grace. He is the Rahmatul-'ālamīn (the Mercy and Compassion of all the universes) who creates, protects, and sustains. He protects the good and destroys evil. He is the One who can change the destiny that has been written. He has the power to transform what can be transformed. If we praise Him and pray to Him, He can change our destiny and give us long lives. He can forgive and erase our faults and grant us what is good. He, Allah, is the Chieftain of so many different sections. Accepting that Lord of all the universes is the primary secret in our life.

If this acceptance is complete and carried out in the right manner, that will in itself be the pathway to paradise.

That is the path that leads to heaven. The steadfastness of absolute faith (*īmān*) is what opens the path. With certitude and determination, we must follow the path that opens before us; as we proceed on that path, we will realize His threefold function of creation, protection, and sustenance.

If we reach the other shore, we will be sustained. If, when we experience difficulty on the way, we praise Him and focus our intention upon Him, we will be protected. If we cross over to the other shore, all our faults will be forgiven and we will be given sustenance. The demons that come to kill us will be destroyed.

Precious children, my love you. This is why the *kalimah* was given, so that we may accept Allah and His prophets and live together as one family. That is its meaning.

It means that all praise belongs only to Him and there is no Lord other than God. All creations praise Him. The trees, vines, plants, leaves, and flowers give praise to God alone. The flowers give their fragrance to Him. The leaves perform *tasbīh*, glorifying Him. All fruits with their tastes bow to Him in obeisance and receive even greater tastes. The leaves move in obeisance and acquire a beautiful sheen. The grasses bend in remembrance of God (*dhikr*) and receive long lives.

Jeweled lights of my eyes, my love you. The five elements of earth, fire, water, air, and ether will never be destroyed. These elements reappear continuously. We can make fire using a rock. There is fire in the rocks, there is fire in water, there is fire in air, fire in the body, fire in the sky and in the earth. Similarly, water also exists in each of these, as do air and earth. These connections change and the elements return over and over again. They disappear into the earth, and then they emerge from the earth. The water reappears, the air reappears, and the fire reappears. These elements are angels that praise God. Whatever appears in creation is manifested by way of these angels. This is the nature of birth. They are born, they change, they are destroyed, and then they appear once again.

Our base desires (*nafs*) and our five senses are like this, too. They are born as a result of desire, or as a result of attachments. *This* is what is called 'reincarnation'. Reincarnation applies only to the elements, the senses, and the base desires. What is born will die and what dies can be reborn, but this applies only to the elements, the senses, and desire, not to man. It does not apply to a true human being (*insān*). One who is a true human being is born only once, and in the end disappears within God. He appears from and disappears in God. He never dies. True man comes as one of the six kinds of lives, the one that is never born and will never die. This is the soul, the light soul, and whether it goes or stays, it never dies nor is it ever born. It changes.

For example, when you switch on the current, light emerges from a bulb. As soon as you switch the current off, the light returns to the battery. Does this mean the light is dead? The light is not dead. It is contained in the body, in the five elements. On the Day of Judgment the light of the soul reemerges. As soon as the body is in the grave, the light changes. It changes and leaves, returning to *Allāhu*.

The soul is never born and will never die. It has eternal life (*hayāt*). It is the five elements that die. They will die and be reborn over and over again, assuming four hundred trillion, ten thousand kinds of forms. Earth, fire, water, air, and ether will continue to return but the soul is a light. Of the six kinds of lives, this is the sixth life, the life of a true human being. It is the grace of God and a resplendent light. It has neither birth nor death.

Everything else will be born and eventually die. Each will come with a certain taste and when that taste changes it will leave. First a flower becomes an unripe fruit, then it ripens and becomes sweet or bitter or sour. An unripe fruit

lasts only until it attains the flavor of a ripe fruit. Then it falls
to the ground and its seeds grow again. This is the way with
everything that appears, develops a taste, and then falls.
Desire is like this. Desire enters each thing that is desired in
the world, attains fulfillment, then dies and falls, only to
reappear and start over again.

The grass and the weeds are the same. There are also
certain trees which when you cut them down will recover
and grow again. But there are some trees that will not grow
once they have been cut down. In the same way, any man
who has cut the world away from himself will not live within
the world. He will neither be born again nor will he grow
again. But, the man who has not succeeded in cutting away
the world and continues to be enmeshed in the five elements
will live in the world and will return over and over and over
again to this world. He will be born over and over again, one
hundred and five million times, until finally he ends up as a
worm in hell. We should reflect on this. We should let go of
things that change, and instead change ourselves and progress
from one level to the next. That is our work.

If we want to travel by bus from the city to our home,
we may have to change buses several times. Sometimes we
may be able to find a direct bus; at other times we will have
to take several buses. Similarly, in our life we may have to
change buses many times in order to reach our destination.
However, some buses do go directly. If we can find a good
sheikh, a man of wisdom, such a person will be like an
express bus that will take us directly, without wasting time
on the journey. If we do not find a man of wisdom, we may
become caught in the many religions, scriptures, races,
philosophies, and the differences of 'mine' and 'yours'. There
are several such companies, and if we get on their buses, they
will only take us part of the way, up to a certain point. They
do not have a license to take us further. So we will have to

find another bus from a different company which will take us to yet another point, and we will have to repeat this process over and over again. A bus that goes straight through is very rare, but such a one does exist. If we find such a bus, it will carry us directly across.

To do this, you need a sheikh of good wisdom. You have to find such a sheikh. This does not mean that you should go searching for a person with titles and positions. He will not live with titles or honors. There are many, many people who like to give themselves titles such as *amīr* or *khātim* and say that they are great. He has no such title. Titles are for the military. In armies around the world, the more people you kill the more medals you get. A person might have rows and rows of medals and hats, but what are they for, what do they represent? They are for the number of ships he has sunk, the number of planes he has destroyed, and the number of people he has killed. They are awarded for how many people he has killed, not for how many people he has helped. This is not the kind of title we should search for.

Everyone seems to be seeking titles and fame, and it seems that the more sins and evil we commit, the more fame, respect, and titles we are given. Whereas, if we do something good, if we go along the path of goodness, all we get from the world is rejection. But the more the world pushes us away, the more we can withdraw from it, and as we withdraw more and more, we will find peace. Then we can proceed easily. Instead of having to push our way through a crowd slowly and with great difficulty, the crowd will push us away and we can find the path and proceed on our own. Then it will become easier for us to be free of the obstacles of the world and move on. We will not receive any titles. Instead people will continue beating on us. Those beatings will be the medals we receive from the world. When they beat us on our backs it gives us strength; it strengthens our backbone. And if this backbone, our certitude and faith, remains strong, we can proceed still further.

We should proceed with faith and certitude, not with medals that are attained by killing others. If you trust in medals and wish to acquire great titles and honors, then you should join the army, the navy, or some such organization. Or you can claim to be the leader of a religion, a race, the leader of a philosophy, a king, a military commander, or the ruler of the world, of a city, and so on. If you do this, you will be given more and more titles.

But on this path there are no titles. There is nothing here that will strangle us, only things that will set us free. If at some time titles do grab us, they will choke us until we cannot breathe and we will die. Before these titles tighten around us and kill us, we must find the things that will set us free so that we may proceed easily.

This is the only way that we can proceed without difficulty. This is the path to the freedom of the soul. Therefore, all of us must proceed on this path, protecting ourselves while giving love to others, and protecting them as we would protect ourselves. We must proceed giving comfort to others, sharing our food with others, sharing our water with others, loving our neighbors as ourselves, and making all mankind our relatives, our brothers and sisters. We must proceed making everyone our loved ones and helping them become those who trust in God, and then go together on this path as the followers of God, as the representatives of God, as the children of the One Father.

This is the medal God gives us. It is not really a medal but a model that God makes out of us, a beautiful example. If we can become that model, that will be the medal we earn from Him. We must live as the model of God's beautiful qualities; we must live as the model of a truly realized human being (*insān kāmil*). Such a person will be the most beautiful in the community of mankind. In his qualities, in his actions, his conduct, his disposition, his love, and his way of embracing other lives, he will be more beautiful than any other being. The exaltedness of a person with such beauty is the medal that God gives.

We must obtain that medal. And this is what we must give back to Him. When our Father asks, "What have you earned in life?" we will say, "This is what I have earned," and we will place the medal around His neck. We will take the medal from around our neck and put it on His neck. We must fashion this model within us. If, instead, we seek titles, we will be murderers and wrongdoers, and at one time we will be questioned for this. This sheikh will not come, that *sayyid* will not come—no one will come there. Who would come there? God's questions are going to come in the grave:

"Who is your *Rabb*, your Lord? Who is your God?"
"Allah." We have to say, "Allah."
"Who is your Prophet? Whose follower are you?"
"I am a follower of Muhammad ﷺ."
"What is your *qiblah*?"
"The *Ka'bah*."
"To whose family do you belong?"
"I am from the family of Abraham ﷺ."
"Whose child are you?"
"I am the child of Adam ﷺ."
"Who is your *imām*?"
"The Qur'an is my *imām*. Truth is my *imām*."
"To what group do you belong? Who are your relatives?"
"I belong to the group called the *mu'mins*, the ones who are pure, who accept God in purity. Those are the ones I call my relatives."

We cannot mention any other name at that time. These are the questions you are going to be asked. *"As-salāmu 'alaikum."* These are the words we have to say in the grave.

This is what they say Munkar and Nakīr ☺ will ask. I am not dead yet. I did not die, give the answers and come back. I died many times, but I came back without being involved with questions; I came back without being questioned. But questions might be asked at that time. They say, that this is how they will ask. I died; they didn't ask me these questions. Therefore, because it is said that God said this, I am saying these words. They didn't ask me these questions. They didn't ask me. We have to believe this is true. God said we have to believe. I believe. I accept and believe. Therefore, no matter how many titles we have here, nothing will come of it. The truth is accepting His angels, His heavenly beings, accepting the prophets, accepting Him, accepting prayer, praying to He who is One, accepting the *qiblah*, accepting the *imām*—the *imām* is Truth, the Qur'an. Like this, there will come a time when we have to say each word. But nothing else in the world will come. None of these titles will come.

Therefore, what should we search for in this world? We need to search for wisdom and we need to find a father of wisdom. This is what the *Rasūlullāh* ☺ has said. The Qur'an has been given into our own hands. Where is the Qur'an? The Qur'an is the form of man, the *sūratul-insān*. This form is made out of the twenty-eight Arabic letters, and this form of the Qur'an is referred to as *Sūratur-Rahmān, Sūratul-Fātihah, Sūratul-Qur'ān,* and *Sūrat Yā Sīn.* This Qur'an is here. It is the form (*sūrat*) of man.

God explains this Qur'an in 6,666 different ways and through countless words and *ahādīth*. The entire Qur'an is within the twenty-eight letters. Having provided all these explanations, God said that if all the water in the world was turned into ink and all the wood made into pens, and if you dipped the pens into the ink and wrote about the Qur'an, you still could not complete writing about it or discovering the entirety of its meaning. Therefore, this is not easy.

One who is a human being (*insān*) is the Qur'an. Even if all the water in the world were turned into ink, it would be impossible to assess or describe the state of his mind, his wisdom, and his actions. It is impossible to describe it in totality, because he is the Qur'an. It cannot be assessed or evaluated. Within this form of the Qur'an, man has the beautiful radiant form of a perfected being (*insān kāmil*).

Only when man understands that inner form known as *kāmil* and *insān* will he know what this Qur'an truly is. This Qur'an made of these twenty-eight letters was explained through the medium of 6,666 verses to the *Rasūlullāh*, the Messenger of God, Prophet Muhammad ﷺ. Man was told, "Investigate and analyze yourself through these verses. One who knows himself will know his Lord." God has said, "If you know yourself, then you will never face defeat. You will see Me. Once you know yourself, no disaster will ever befall you in this world, or anywhere. You can see Me."

One who knows himself will see his Leader. *Allāhu taʻālā Nāyan* (the Lone One who rules and sustains) exists as the Qur'an. It is to understand this that the verses (*āyats*) were sent down. God has praised the greatness of *insān*. In the divine realm of *ākhirah*, God praised man in front of the angels. He placed a radiant light before them all and said, "Look at this! Is there anyone among you who can accept this light?" The brilliance of the light swallowed the lights of all the other beings.

All the lights said, "We cannot accept this light. O Allah, it will swallow and overshadow our light. You alone, O God, can accept this light, not any of us."

It is at this point that the earth came forward and said, "I will accept this light."

And God said, "O earth, you have sought your own ruin."

The earth accepted the light, the Qur'an, and that is why it is hidden by the five elements. It is because the earth accepted the light that the Qur'an lies within the body made of earth. The 6,666 explanations are within, and we must understand them. We must understand, "Who is man? Who is God? What is the world? What is the hereafter (ākhirah)? What is heaven and what is hell? What is goodness and what is evil? What is right (khair) and what is wrong (sharr)? What is permissible (halāl) and what is impermissible (harām)? What is the essence (dhāt) and what are the manifestations (sifāt)?" We have come to this world to understand the explanations to these questions.

All this is contained within our form (sūrat). This is why the Rasūl ﷺ has said that it is impossible to measure the depth of the Qur'an, because it is impossible to discover its entire content. If a man cannot even complete this, how can he finish learning the 6,666 inner explanations! In addition to this, Allah has given countless teachings (ahādīth). How can one finish learning these?

The Rasūl ﷺ said, "I could not have said anything that was not spoken by Allah. My tongue would not have spoken any word that Allah has not spoken. Whether by night or by day, I have not revealed anything that was not given by Allah." This is stated in the Qur'an and the ahādīth. Like this, if man transforms himself into the wealth of God (daulat), then what comes from his tongue will be the word of God. But if he transforms himself into the wealth of the earth, the dunyā, then the words that come will be the words of the five elements. Those are the only words that will come.

The words of man can have two meanings. When he turns to God, only God's words will be spoken, but when he turns to the world, then the different aspects of the world will be spoken by his tongue. When a man turns toward truth, his inner heart (*qalb*) will be radiant and will resplend with perfect peace and equality. But when he is agitated, he will have evil qualities, grief, sorrow, and separations. These four will join together, stir up trouble, and wail.

Each child should reflect on this and understand. God, the unique, unparalleled One who rules and sustains (*Allāhu ta'ālā*), is the Great One. He is One of immeasurable grace and incomparable love. He has created man (*insān*) in a most exalted manner. But you have not understood that your form, your *sūrat*, is the Qur'an. Allah gave the meaning of this, but you have not understood that. This is why the *Rasūl* ﷺ said, "Go even unto China to learn divine knowledge (*'ilm*)." If you really want to understand yourself, the Qur'an, and these explanations, find a man of wisdom, because it is only through such a man that you can realize the true value of this. It is through his wisdom that you can understand.

A man of wisdom will not have any titles; he will be hidden somewhere. He would have made himself silent. But a man who has no wisdom will brag and display his titles. A wise one, a true man, will be like a ripe fruit that is hidden by a cluster of leaves, out of sight. There will be some people like this in the world. But there are others who will act as though they know everything. They will parade around proclaiming their titles, "I am an *amīr*, I am an *'ālim*, I am a great one. I know everything." Some go on pilgrimage (*hajj*) to Mecca. It is said that out of one million people who go on pilgrimage, only one will have truly fulfilled this duty. In times past the voice of God would come and announce the name of the one who had achieved this state of true *hajj*. Everyone would rush to pay their respects to that person, thinking, "Maybe we will be blessed and attain peace if we can touch his feet or hands." But things are different in modern times. Now, in certain countries, even before going on pilgrimage, some people add the word "Hajjiyar" to their name and order their name plaques to be made before they return. *Hajjiyar* is the title for those who have been on *hajj,* and *Hajji Hajjiyar* is the title for those who have gone more than once. Even before they leave they ask for these plaques to be made for their door. Then they go on pilgrimage. While there, they use the time to arrange some business deals, and when they return they hang out their "Hajjiyar" signs.

Many people go to Mecca to receive titles, but a man of wisdom will be different. For him the *hajj* is a journey to meet God, and when he goes the world will have died within him. He is not dead. The world is dead, his base desires (*nafs*) are dead, and his attachments are dead. He will make all the sins he has committed die by making supplication (*du'ā'*) to Allah.

The fifth obligatory duty (*fard*) of Islam, *hajj,* or pilgrimage, is for a person to put to death these things within him. To make all that he has done and all that he has gathered in his life die and to attain eternal life (*hayāt*) is *hajj.* From then on he no longer possesses the world, the *dunyā.* To go to Allah and receive the radiance of Allah's eternal life is *hajj.* To obtain the wealth of Allah (*daulat*) is *hajj.* To worship only Him, to love only Him, to praise only Him, and to sing only of Him is *hajj,* because in that state only Allah remains; the world no longer exists.

Who is there that has performed that kind of *hajj* in this day? Nowadays the *hajj* is used to attain titles and to do business. That is all. But a man of wisdom does not search for titles. He makes the world die within himself, he makes the 'I' die within him, and he makes desire die within him. He makes himself a slave to Allah, and in this way he makes his life into an eternal life (*hayāt*). Earlier he was dead within the world and within his desires, but now, having made them die

within him, he has attained freedom; he has made his life
eternal and has become a slave to Allah. These are the titles
that a man of wisdom earns as he completely surrenders to
the feet of Allah. Surrendering to Allah and becoming Allah's
slave—these are the titles impressed on his inner heart.

Anyone who attains this state will not face the questioning and suffering in the grave. Why? Only as long as the
world (dunyā) is within him will he be questioned, but once
the world dies within him there will be no questions for him.
As long as the world is within him, he has death, but if he
makes the world die, he has no death. He attains liberation.
These are the benefits we must obtain.

My precious children, every child, we must reflect on
this. My daughters, my sons, brothers, sisters, granddaughters, grandsons, and all my precious children, my love you.
My beloved jeweled lights, the riches we have to attain are
not the praise we receive in this world. We must become
those who will give Allah's praise to Allah and receive His
wealth. We must give to Allah that which belongs to Him.
We must bow down in obeisance to Him, surrender completely to Him, and become His slaves. Then we must
become a true child to our Father.

From the time we were in the womb until now, our
Father has done everything for us. He created us, protected
us, and brought us up even when our own father and mother
forgot us. He has always given us food and nourishment. He
protected us and watched over us. Such is our Father, Almighty Allah. He has done everything for us thus far and
now the time has come for us to earn and to give Him
something in return. What food can we give God? We have
to work hard and attain His qualities, His conduct, His
benevolence, His words, His actions, the duties He performs, and the words He speaks. We must develop all of
these within us in the same way that He does. This is what

we must earn and return to Him. This is the food that we can give Him. We must become His slaves. We must become His children. This is the wealth we must earn henceforth and hand over to our Father.

Everything we have thought of so far has been given to us by our Father, and now we must strive to give Him what He is thinking of. That is His property. Only when this state is formed within us will we earn the right to be the child of our Father. We will be free of all blemishes and evil, and goodness will come to us. Paradise and the world will both be heaven to us. The good qualities will dispel the darkness of the world, making this world heaven and the hereafter (ākhirah) more precious. The beauty of our life will become even greater. Our words and our actions will become radiant, our conduct exalted. Our gaze, our thoughts, and our intentions will be filled with the wealth of God (daulat). We will attain a state where Allah's prophets and saints become our relatives who will come to meet us and talk with us.

May we affirm that God, the unique, unparalleled One who rules and sustains (Allāhu ta'ālā Nāyan), is the benevolent One who bestows grace on us. May we accept this and surrender only to Him. May we search for the things that He wants us to seek, find them, take them to Him, and make our Father peaceful. If we perform prayer (vanakkam), worship through service ('ibādat), ritual prayer (toluhai), the constant remembrance of God (dhikr), and complete concentration on God (fikr), we will bring great happiness to our Father. If we have His qualities, His actions and behavior and bow down in obeisance and worship and if we take all those things which belong to Him and give them to Him, we will bring great happiness to our Father. It will give Him peace, and He will give us peace in return. He will embrace us and kiss us, and that will be our peace.

My precious jeweled lights, my love you. Every child

should reflect on this, and having reflected you must progress on this path. Do not search for titles, praise, respect, and status. Titles belong to murderers and those who commit evil. When people wage war and kill people, they get titles. Do not do what is bad in order to attain titles. Do what is good and seek only for the qualities of God. Hand those qualities back to our Father and receive His beauty, His light, and His compassion. This is what we should try to do. Both you and I should do this. Precious children, this is the greatest fortune we can ever attain, and we must all come forward in quest of this goal.

Precious jeweled lights of my eyes, if there is anything wrong, any fault, in what I have now spoken, please forgive me. If I have said anything without understanding, please forgive me. In truth, it is not humiliating to ask for forgiveness; it is a sign of exaltedness in our life. To think, "Oh, these are small people, why should I ask forgiveness from them," is not an agreeable way of thinking. Forgiveness is an exalted thing, an elevated thing, but its manner is always low and humble. Those things that are low in value, however, will always try to rise up and show you that they are high. But they have no real value.

The more you make yourselves humble and ask for forgiveness, the more your true exaltedness is realized. Humility is a sign of exaltedness. The preface of *Īmān-Islām* is patience (*sabūr*), contentment and gratitude (*shakūr*), having trust in God (*tawakkul*), and praising Him for everything that happens to us, saying, "*Al-hamdu lillāh!*" Therefore, without feeling shame, ask forgiveness whenever necessary. This will be good. Allah, the Lone One who rules and sustains (*Allāhu ta'ālā Nāyan*) will protect you and me.

He is the One who has forbearance. The world and its people do not have much patience. They do not forgive easily, but God will forgive. Say, "I seek forgiveness from

Allah, the Supreme (*Astaghfirullāhal-'azīm*)," and He will
forgive. The people of this world do not have much forbearance. They will magnify one wrong tenfold and give us more
and more suffering in return. If we can ask for forgiveness
before this happens, they will be appeased and we can
escape. That will be good.

My love you, my precious children, this is how it is. If
there is anything wrong in what I have said or in what I have
done, I ask for forgiveness. Please forgive me. *Āmīn. Āmīn.*
May the peace of God be with all of you. May His wealth
and His grace and all that is His be with all of you. *As-salāmu
'alaikum wa rahmatullāhi wa barakātahu kulluhu. Āmīn.*

June 24, 1984

PART TWO

Questions and Answers

WHY DIDN'T YOU THINK
OF THIS BEFORE?

———⋯◦⟨∞⟩◦⋯———

I do not know where they went.
  This person is not here,
And neither is that one.
This person's wealth is not here,
And neither is that one's.

Everyone who has come here,
The young and the elderly,
The newborn babies, the old men,
And those in the prime of their life
Are like the leaves, flowers, and fruit
That blossom, then fade and fall from the tree.
Everyone who has been born
Has died, rolled away, and been buried
    in the earthly world.

Blood ties, attachments, and bondages,
Loved ones and trusted ones, our wealth
    and possessions,
Though we might have claimed rights to all these,
They did not tell us when they were leaving.
They did not say, "I am going,"
Neither did they say, "I am staying."

No one knows where they have gone,
There is not a word, not a breath about it.
When they left, they did not say anything.
Even though we wept and begged,
All they did was run away.
Rivers of tears were running from our eyes,
And they said nothing.

Everyone who came has gone.
Everyone we saw before,
We see no longer.
The few who are left
Now sing and weep.

Those who have gone no longer own any property,
Houses, cows, or goats.
As soon as someone goes,
Everyone else comes running, saying,
"These are mine. That is mine;
    give me my property."
They punch and pinch each other.
They roll on the ground.
They break each other's heads, arms, and legs,
Trying to grab what they can.
In the end nothing is left.

We cannot see those who went,

Nor the ones who accumulated wealth,

Nor the ones we were used to seeing before,

Nor the ones who fashioned things in different ways.

We cannot see the One who sees us,

The One who created everything in perfect order.

A person who has lived his life trusting this world

Will see nothing.

He will have no helper.

He will not know the place to which he will go.

Having forgotten his Father,

He lies fascinated in the ocean of this world.

None of those who were fascinated

By the ocean of this world,

None of those who leaped and played,

Danced and wandered in this ocean, are left.

Those who have yet to arrive, will arrive.

Those who came here earlier, will leave.

Those who have yet to come, will also go.

Those who came before, have left.

Those who are here, are here for now.

This is the state the world is in.

The world has been decorated, this is its state.

But the world does not speak.

Man tries to make it speak.

He decorates it and makes it beautiful.
He adorns himself for the dance,
He beautifies himself and sings and dances as
    an actor.
He tries to bewitch those who come here, those who
    are still alive,
With the fascination of the sixty-four arts, the
    sixty-four sexual games.
He tries to hold them spellbound with his forty-two
    acts and dances.
He sings and dances in this world in order to
    fascinate others.
This world is an act, and man is but an actor in it.
As an actor he does this dance.
He is an actor and this world is a stage.
His adornments are the sixty-four sexual games,
His jewelry is the sixty-four arts.
He is fascinated by the frenzied celebration of lust
    and sexual love.
He loses his modesty and wisdom.
He is trapped in a house of illusion.
Tangled in mental and physical visions,
He stumbles, falls, and cries out for help.

After the dance is over,
After the song comes to an end,
When his tongue flaps uselessly

And his eyes grow dim,

When sounds are blocked from his ears

And his body is left weak, without strength,

He reflects and weeps about everything he wanted,

Everything he decorated.

"It was all useless!" he howls.

"Everything I saw was false," he yells.

"I have no helper," he wails.

"I was deceived," he cries.

Only at the end does he realize this.

"No one is here to help me," he wails aloud in grief.

This is the life of man.

"Why didn't you think of this before, O my mind?

Why didn't you think of this before?"

This is what happens to everyone.

Look at this.

You, too, have been deceived by this,

This is what has happened.

Look at the five and six duties[1] in your heart.

If you know these and search for them with wisdom,

Then six joys will come to you,

Six sweet tastes will come into you,

Six levels of wisdom will dawn.

---

1. See *furud* in glossary.

The resonance of Allāhu will descend upon you.
His qualities, His actions, and His behavior will
come within you
As your Teacher, your Grace, your Father.
He will teach and advise you from within,
And you will never lack anything.
Know this, my life,
Realize this.
Āmīn!

November 11, 1985

5

THE THREE COMPONENTS OF LIFE

———————•·❨∞❩·•———————

Bawa Muhaiyaddeen: When the sperm joins the ovum and conception takes place, what comes is the *ānmā*. Then the earth, fire, water, and air cover the *ānmā* in the form of flesh and skin.

Question: What is the meaning of *ānmā*?

Bawa Muhaiyaddeen: *Ānmā* is the essence of the senses. It is the essence of the earth, fire, and water that form the body. In the first month, on the third day after conception, that power known as *ānmā*, the essence of the elements, joins with the embryo. Then the embryo starts to move. In the second month, the *āvi* enters into this. That is the pure spirit, or vapor. By the end of the third month the soul is sent within that pure spirit and the embryo's movement increases. Within ninety days, slowly the pure spirit pushes the soul in from above and life becomes evident in the fetus.

Thus, at the end of three months, three sections or forces are present—the spirit or essence of the elements, the pure spirit, and the soul. They are commonly spoken of as one thing, but these three are different from one another, and they each enter the embryo at a different time. First comes the essence of the elements, the *ānmā*; second comes the pure spirit, the *āvi*; and third comes the soul, the light. By the third month the fetus has reached this point of growth; the soul has been pushed in by the pure spirit and brought down into the embryo.

When a man dies these three leave in the same order

that they came. First there will be a flutter, next a gasp, then
the eyes will look up and drop down. These three forces of
life leave in these three ways; they do not leave the body at
the same time. First, the essence of the elements, the *ānmā*,
ceases functioning and dies, starting at the toes and continuing up to the heart. It is the *ānmā* dying that causes the rattle
in the chest. The *ānmā* works through air, bile, and phlegm.

The *āvi*, the pure spirit, functions with the soul, or *rūh*.
When the body is dying, the heat and power of the pure
spirit diminishes. First, the *ānmā*, or the essence of the elements, dies; then second, the *āvi* diminishes. When the *ānmā*
dies, the rattling sound lessens and only movement remains.
Then movement lessens and only the heat of the *āvi* remains.
Next that heat of the pure spirit diminishes, and then finally
the life, the light, the *rūh*, leaves. The person opens his eyes
for a moment and in a flash the light, the life, is gone.

So, there are three components of life in man. One is
the power of the five elements called *ānmā*, the essence of the
senses. It works through air, bile, and phlegm which are
connected to the elements. The second is the *āvi*, the pure
spirit, which works in connection with the soul through
heat. And the third is the soul itself, the *rūh*, which works
through the light, the power.

Question: Is the soul everywhere in the body or is it just in
one place?

Bawa Muhaiyaddeen: It cannot be described. It is spread
everywhere. All three operate everywhere in the body. You
can estimate the magnitude or quantity of the *ānmā* and *āvi*,
but you cannot assess the station of the soul, *rūh*. One does
not know where it dwells. Nobody knows what it is or where
it is. The *ānmā*, or the essence of the elements, can be assessed. It works through air, bile, and phlegm. The heat, the
pure vapor, *āvi*, can also be assessed, but the soul, the light,

cannot; it is connected to God. Jibrīl ⊕ can be ascertained as the āvi and Adam ⊕ who is the ānmā can be ascertained; but the soul cannot. You cannot ascertain what it is.

It is said that there are sixteen kinds of lives in the body. There is the earth life, fire life, water life, air life, and ether life. Then there is ānmā, the essence of the elements, āvi, the pure vapor, and the soul, or light life. These are the eight heavens or eight stations. Only after understanding these eight can we know where the soul is.

The soul has no shadow. God has no shadow, no form, no shape. God is a power. Only the Qutbiyyat Nūr, the resplendence of divine wisdom, can understand and know this. It is a light. One light has to go and turn on the other light. When the light of the Qutbiyyat touches the light life, a magnetic power draws them into one another. It is at this point that the soul can be understood. There is a power that draws these two lights together. That is God. These three components are present in every life. The earth lives also have it, animals also have this, water lives have this, and air lives also have these three. Worms, birds, every life has these three sections.

Question: Within which of these three are the base desires, the nafs?

Bawa Muhaiyaddeen: They are connected to the ānmā. The ānmā is the essence of the body. From the body and the five elements come the base desires, the nafs. The essence filtered from these elements is ānmā. The nafs come from the five elements.

Question: If one does not succeed in becoming a true man, what happens? Do the nafs come back to this world, to the dunyā?

Bawa Muhaiyaddeen: The nafs and ānmā remain behind in the world. A flashlight has a bulb, a glass that covers it, and a battery inside the case. The current is inside the battery, and when we press the switch the light comes on. When we turn the switch off the light goes off; the current returns into the battery and the light is no longer seen. When the switch was on, the current emerged and the light was seen. When the switch was turned off, the light could not be seen, nor the current that produces the light. But we could still see the battery, the bulb, the glass, and the switch.

The soul is like this. God's power is within it and works within it. When God's power is switched on, the soul shines. When that power is switched off, the soul goes back to Him. You can still see the earth, the *nafs*, the body, and whatever work the man did while alive, just as you can still see the light, the glass, the switch, the battery, the springs, and the bulb. All of these can be seen, but not the soul. The soul belongs to God. The current, the power that brings forth the light, is not seen, but it is there within the battery.

Man can see all the sections of the body. They are all here, but the section of the soul, the *rūb*, is operated by the switch that God has. When He puts it on, the soul comes into being. When He turns it off, the soul returns to Him. It goes back into Him. Everything else remains here, but that soul does not remain. It disappears in God.

You cannot equate the light life to the other elemental lives; they belong to the world and the soul belongs to God. The battery, the aluminum case, the bulb, the glass, the springs, the metal pieces, and the switch are things that are visible. The senses and what we see here are like these parts of the flashlight. It is within these that the soul is kept. When the switch is turned on, it comes. When the switch is turned off, it goes. It cannot be seen. It works through the means of the switch. That is the soul.

The *ānmā*, the essence of the elements, works through the form of air, bile, and phlegm. It can be assessed by the pulse. Heat or the *āvi*, the pure vapor, can also be ascertained by the pulse, but the soul cannot. Its presence cannot be detected.

Within certain places of the earth there is a magnetic current. If an object made of iron, like a knife or an ax, falls on such a spot, the current in the earth will pull on it and hold it fast. It will be stuck to the ground. When you pull on the object, it will not come loose. No one was even aware of the presence of that magnetic force in the earth until the iron object fell upon it.

Similarly, the power of the soul is present within the body. When wisdom touches upon the soul, the soul will hold onto it. Then you will know that the soul exists. You will then know that the soul has a force similar to that in a magnet. The soul is spread in the body just like the magnetic power is spread throughout the earth. But first, the appropriate thing must fall upon it, and only then will you realize the power of the soul.

June 20, 1973

6

What Happens When We Die?

———————————————

Question: What happens immediately after a person dies? What happens at the moment of death?

Bawa Muhaiyaddeen: If you beat a bull to death or cut its throat, what does it do when it dies? It stops making any noise, but it is still suffering. On the outside you see its body trembling, and inside all its parts are quivering; every nerve, muscle, and tissue is twitching.

In the same way, every quality that is within you and each of the five kinds of lives (earth life, fire life, water life, air life, and ether life, or illusion (*māyā*)) lose their power when the rays (elemental souls) are being taken away. Unable to emit any sound on the outside, all the thoughts within go on quivering and twitching until they finally subside. At this time, some people see the fire known as hell. You will see whatever demon that you nourished and raised. All your thoughts will appear as demons and ghosts and dogs coming to bite you, tear you apart, and devour you. They will take a form and appear before your eyes shouting, "Hey, you rascal, are you leaving me and going away? Who is there left for me to inhabit now? Don't go! Come back!" Like this every part within you will cause you untold agony and suffering.

At this time, when they are still partly conscious, some people babble incomprehensibly, "That is going. This is coming. Demons are coming at me! Ghosts are coming at me! Fire is coming at me! Somebody is coming to kill me!"

Some do not speak, but tears flow from their eyes. Some seem to scream at the slightest thing. Water oozes out of some people's mouths, their tongues hang out, or their noses start running. Some people tremble and their bodies go into convulsions. Some people have rattling noises in their throats. Many different kinds of actions and sufferings will occur in the body at that time.

At that time, all the sins and evils you have committed, all the murders that you have committed, will be seen in front of you, like the hallucinations you have from LSD. If you have killed somebody, you will see that before you. If you have caused harm to somebody or if you have scolded somebody, that will come and stand before you.

Everything a person did before, all the thoughts he had, will come and surround him at that time. These are the only things that he will see. He may not be able to speak, but he will see all these things as his end approaches. He does not die immediately. These things quiet down, little by little, as his life subsides.

The soul will remain with you until you are placed in the grave. Until your soul departs, everything you experienced before, all the singing and dancing, all the shouting and drinking, and all the attachments to your relatives will be seen by your eyes and heard by your ears, but it will be as though you were under anesthesia. You will not be able to talk or move, but you will be aware of everything. Before an operation, you are given anesthesia so you will not be conscious of the pain, but your body remains aware of what is being done to it. In the same way, you cannot speak or shout, you cannot move, you cannot do anything, but an awareness within your body knows what is happening. Until you are placed in the grave and covered with earth and everyone has taken seven steps away, you will know everything. After that, the angels will come and ask you certain questions and have you write down everything you have done.

At this point the life leaves the body and the body begins to disintegrate. But there is an inner body which will face the questioning. That form is made up of the thoughts, emotions, desires, shadows, demons, satans, and ghosts that were deceiving and consuming your body all your life. You were merely a servant carrying out its commands. It is similar to somebody hiring another person to commit a murder. This inner body is the one who is the real culprit, the real murderer. It committed all the sins and ate the wealth of the world, so it must answer the questions and receive the judgment. It must face the real suffering; the outer body will only have to experience a little suffering, because it just followed orders.

If you have done evil during your life, you will see the evil qualities which you have nurtured. But if you have done good, you will see only the vision of God. You will see all the angels and heavenly beings, and the beautiful adornments of the reception awaiting you. You will see the kingdom of heaven with all its beauty and bliss. There will be a welcoming message, "We have been expecting you. We have been awaiting you. Come, please come." That is how it will be seen, as two different sections. Each one of us will know at that time, even though we cannot speak.

The inner body treats the outer body as a slave and functions from within. Our cravings, base desires, demons, and ghosts work from inside us. A few months ago, you were very worried about your apartment, about the rent, about what they had done to it, and so on. You were almost going crazy worrying about it. If you had died at that time, that is what you would have seen in front of your eyes. This is how it is.

March 23, 1979

7

WHAT DETERMINES THE TIME OF DEATH?

———————···◁∞▷···———————

Question: What determines the time of death?

Bawa Muhaiyaddeen: There is a system, or set of rules, an agreement which governs the existence of whatever appears. This system is present in each embryo and determines when each living thing will blossom, function, and fade. Flowers and fruits are governed by this same system. This is what determines the size each fruit will attain and how long it will last. Likewise, there is an agreement as to how long a pregnancy will last and how long it will take for an embryo to develop. This is what they say. Everything happens according to this agreement. For example, some flowers last for four days, some for three days, some for only one day, while others last for a week. There are fruits that ripen in three months and others that ripen in one month.

   Like that, each seed has a specific agreement. The plant that emerges functions in accordance with that destiny, and its flowers will fade and fall off at the destined time. However, some plants might be beaten and blown by the wind or destroyed by fire or water. According to the seasons, they may be destroyed or broken in different ways.

   In the same way, man's seed might depart according to the time that is decreed by that agreement, or it might depart by an accident, or as a result of his own actions. The air in the body might become too much, the heat of the fire might be too much, and maybe the water becomes too much. Or maybe the gas increases, or illusion (*māyā*), the

cravings, and the desires become excessive. Or the blood
may increase, or the fat in the body may become too much.
Due to various reasons like this, an accident might occur.

Just as flowers and fruits get beaten down by the wind
or the rain or destroyed by the heat, man is also like a crop.
The whole world is a farm. Creation, that is, whatever has
appeared or manifested, is like a cultivated crop. Each creation has an agreement. Some follow the agreement, while
others are beaten by the five elements and fall before their
time. This is what we call the time limit (kālam). Some seeds
are fertilized at night and some seeds are formed in the day.
Some flowers bloom by day and some bloom by night. Some
flowers give off their fragrance in the daytime, while others
smell nice in the night. Some creations can see well in the
night, and others can see well in the daytime. There are
some creations that can see well both in the daytime and in
the night as long as there is some light. Humans can do this,
and so can cats. There are, however, some cats that cannot
see in the daylight but can see in the night. This is the way
it is.

There are different varieties in creation, each following
the course of the agreement placed in the seed at the time of
their appearance. When that agreement is over, then the
fruit dies or falls. It either becomes ripe or is spoiled before it
ripens. We say that the fruit fell; it was either beaten by the
wind or it became ripe, matured, and fell. The same things
happen to the physical body of man. However, the inner
man is different. There is a portion within man that was
never born and will never die. That is a power; that is the
soul. Once you understand this, you will not have any more
questions.

What happens to the body at the time of death is
similar to a person being given chloroform before an operation. The five elements will know what is happening. The
person lies there gaping and lifeless but still aware of what is

happening. And as soon as he is placed under the earth, the earth takes its section, water takes its own, air takes its portion, and illusion (*māyā*) takes its own. This is what people say. I don't know.

If I had studied all this, why would I be here? There would be no reason for me to be here.

July 28, 1977

8

How Do You Die in a State of True Faith?

———————··◁∞▷··———————

Question: When you know the body is going to die, what is the proper way to die? How do you die in a state of *īmān* (absolute faith, certitude, and determination)?

Bawa Muhaiyaddeen: What dies is the body composed of the five elements: earth, fire, water, air, and ether. Originally the body wrapped around to form a covering for the soul, but now it just dissolves, goes back to the earth, and dissipates into its separate components. When it re-forms again, it takes another birth.

Adam (☉) is the earth, Mīkā'īl (☉) is water, 'Izrā'īl (☉) is fire, Isrāfīl (☉) is wind, and the mind is ether. When the body is laid in the ground, each of the elements absorbs what belongs to it. Earth absorbs the part of the body that is earth, water absorbs the water, fire absorbs the fire, and air absorbs the air. The mind which contains the base desires (*nafs*), the lights, and the glitters is taken by the ether. This is the way the elements take back what is due to them. This is an ongoing process. The elements are separated and absorbed, and then they roll together again to form another body. Then when that body dies, this process is repeated. The body takes form in the elements, is nourished by the elements, and is finally absorbed by the elements.

Question: What I guess I'm really asking is how do you escape? You know this is going to happen so you have to escape the whole process.

Bawa Muhaiyaddeen: The elements of the body do not die. They have eternal life; they are immortal. Illusion, or *māyā*, never dies. The senses never die, they also live forever. They transform themselves into the elements and then unite once again to take form as another body. This process is ongoing. This is what happens with the body, but the soul, wisdom, and light are connected to God. They are His property.

When the Angel of Death comes, it is as if the person is given chloroform. He is not dead. He can still hear all the sounds that the ears normally hear, the perceptions of feeling and awareness are still present, and the brain is still working. All this continues to function, and the body is aware of what is happening, but the person cannot speak.

All the demons and the ghosts will be shouting and crying. All his blood ties who died earlier will call him saying, "Come, come." The father and mother will come. All the spirits of his blood attachments will gather there and call him, "My son, my master, my father." All the connections that were created out of the earth will be around him. The riches, earth, and gold from this world will come. He will be aware of all these things, but he will not be able to open his mouth and speak. He cannot open his eyes and see, due to the effect of the chloroform.

Translator: So the body has not died yet?

Bawa Muhaiyaddeen: No, it is under anesthesia. It stays alive until the questioning in the grave is over.

Question: Does Bawa mean by chloroform that they have embalmed him or something?

Bawa Muhaiyaddeen: No. It is like being under chloroform, due to the injection from the Angel of Death. Until the time he was given that injection, he was shouting, "Oh, my property! My father is coming. My mother is coming. This is coming, that is coming!" The Angel of Death stops all these outer sounds which are caused by the senses. When the chloroform is given, all those senses are driven out and start dancing outside him. The blood ties and all the functions of the body which were conducted by the five elements stand outside the body and shout. All the things that cry about 'my property', 'my relations' have stopped, and they are now standing around wailing and shouting. The only things that remain within are the seven levels of consciousness: feeling, awareness, intellect, judgment, subtle wisdom, divine analytic wisdom, and divine luminous wisdom or light. They watch the senses that are outside and hear everything that is happening. But the person cannot speak. The powers of speech are lost. Only the light of wisdom still lives.

Like this, when the person is taken to the graveyard, he is aware of all that is happening. Once the burial is completed, the two angels, Munkar and Nakīr ☉, will come for the questioning. They will say to the person in the grave, "Wake up!" The chloroform lasts until this point. Then the person gets up and the questioning begins. The twenty-eight letters of the alphabet in the body speak. Each letter is asked, "What did you do? What did you do?" The soul remains in the body until this questioning.

Satan created the fire of cremation in order to send a person to hell even before this questioning can happen. Once the body is burned, the questioning is no longer possible. When the body is cremated, it begins to melt. It remains still until the fire reaches the level of the chest, and at that point, the soul makes the body sit up abruptly. That is why it is the practice to place logs on top of the body during cremation to prevent this from happening. When the fire reaches the chest, the soul leaves the body. The soul, however, cannot be burned by fire and remains untouched, for it has no form. When the fire reaches the person's brain, his skull bursts open. As soon as the brain bursts, wisdom is gone. When the heart bursts, the soul (*rūh*) is gone.

So then where is the kingdom of God in man? It is in the heart. That is heaven. That is God. The heart is the station of God. All that matters is there. This is where God, the soul, and the light of wisdom exist. This is a temple of God which is formed as an atom within an atom, heart within the heart, the *qalb* within the *qalb*. It is within what is within. It cannot be destroyed by the five elements. You must understand this. It can never be destroyed.

Māyā, or illusion, is also something that can never be destroyed. Like the soul, it never dies. *Māyā* is that which belongs to the next birth. It keeps on changing and re-forming and appearing over and over again. But the soul is not something that comes or goes. Once it has become the light, it is the Light. You must focus upon that part which becomes the light. As soon as you see God as God, then that which sees God is God.

Question: What if a person just ignored Munkar and Nakīr (ﷺ) and just did the *kalimah* (*Lā ilāha ill-Allāhu*—There is nothing other than You, O God, only You are Allah)? What if a person just stuck with the *kalimah* and thinking about God and refused to acknowledge these two angels?

Bawa Muhaiyaddeen: The moment you shine the light, the darkness vanishes. Darkness exists only before there is light.

Question: But that is my question, what do you do at that time?

Bawa Muhaiyaddeen: You don't have to do anything about the light. Light is light.

Question: You have to choose one or the other. Don't you?

Translator: You have done your choosing beforehand, haven't you?

Bawa Muhaiyaddeen: Only if darkness and dirt exist is there difficulty. If there is no dirt or darkness, there is only light. You have to keep on cleaning and dusting to prevent the light from being hidden. The dust will try to come and settle on the light. You must clear it.

March 24, 1974

9

THE ANGEL OF DEATH

—————··◁∞▷··—————

Question: A question came to me during the *dhikr* (early morning prayers). The Angel 'Izrā'īl ☾ is spoken of as the Angel of Death. Is that angel associated with the body? What function does 'Izrā'īl ☾ serve within the body, and where does that power reside?

Bawa Muhaiyaddeen: The function he serves is that of destiny (*nasīb*); that which was destined by God. I have seen him with my own eyes. At one time, two of us were flying on a certain mission to look at something. After a while, I left the other person behind and proceeded alone. Then I saw the Angel 'Izrā'īl ☾ seated on a dais, which according to my estimate was two hundred and fifty miles high. I could not see his feet. He was very, very tall. Nearby, there was a tree with leaves in clusters of five or six. All the leaves were shining like stars, and the entire place was glowing with their light. A little further on was another place for judgment. As each soul (*rūh*) came along, it was questioned and then some were allowed to go one way and others were directed to go the other way.

One group was being led up a very high path to heaven, toward the throne of God (*'arsh*). The tree was in close proximity to that throne (*'arsh*). The group going the other way was being sent to hell; they were proceeding downward. This is one of the wonders I saw. I have described it in the book of mystical experiences.

I saw that the Angel of Death had four faces; one face

was black, one was the face of milk, one was the face of fire, the other face was looking at that tree all the time.

I greeted him saying, "As-salāmu 'alaikum, Yā 'Izrā'īl. May the peace of God be with you." Someone had informed me that he was 'Izrā'īl ﷺ. When I looked at him, I found that the whole world was within his eyes, every life was within his eyes. I could not see the world anywhere else except within his eyes.

When I looked at the face of milk, it was a beautiful face. I looked at the face of fire, and it was burning like fire. The black face was very dark, and the fourth face was turned toward the tree. As the souls (rūh) came toward him, he stretched his hand out and grabbed them. There was a huge mountain of souls.

I heard some people scream. 'Izrā'īl ﷺ was looking at them with his gaze of fire. They were shouting, "Please don't burn me. It is like fire." Others were screaming, "Oh, they are cutting me up. They are killing me."

Then I spoke to the Angel of Death. He said, "Look at my eyes. The whole world is within my eyes. I do the work that Allah has given me; this is why I am called 'Izrā'īl. I do only the work given to me by Allah. There is no soul (rūh) that can escape my eyes, even if it is hiding under a stone. No one can hide from me. They cannot live any place where I cannot see."

Then I saw some people with horns on their heads moving about, and their eyes were also like those of 'Izrā'īl ﷺ. They were grabbing people and pulling them across to a big forest, to the place of judgment where the questioning would take place. There was a platform about five feet high, with a veil, and there was a resplendent light coming through that veil. Someone was there. It was he who asked the questions and he who pointed with his hand to show in which direction each person should be taken. Then the people were taken on one path or the other.

I asked the Angel 'Izrā'īl ⊛, "You are always looking toward this tree. What are those lights?"

And he said, "All souls of all lives are on this tree. As soon as a light stops twinkling, we know that a life is ending. The same light that shines here, also shines within each creation. The light represents the light of each individual's soul. Within each person it is the soul, and here it is a light. As soon as a light fades here on this tree, it means that person's allotted food and water (rizq) in the world is over, and it is time for me to bring him back. So I stretch my hand in his direction and summon him here. I have to be looking at this tree every moment to see when a light stops blinking. That is why I must keep a constant watch on this tree.

"The souls of jinns are captured by my face of fire. Evil beings are captured with my black face. Those good people who have the benevolence of God, His thoughts, and His remembrance, I receive with my face of milk. Like the newborn baby suckles milk so gently from the breast without any pain to the mother, I will gently draw the soul of those who are good. I will draw them with the face of milk.

"I am neither above nor below. You cannot say that I am in a particular place. That's the way I am. The world is within every human being, and all worlds can be seen within my eyes. I realize everything that is within me." Then he motioned to me to go further and look, and I saw that the number of people going to heaven were few and the number of people going to hell were many. I was very tired, and so we stopped.

Al-hamdu lillāh. As-salāmu 'alaikum, may the peace of God be with all of you. May God protect all of us.

May 22, 1986

10

What Is the Day of Reckoning?

————•⟨∞⟩•————

Question: What is the difference between the day of destruction and *qiyāmah*?

Bawa Muhaiyaddeen: The day of destruction and *qiyāmah*, the day of reckoning, are both within ourselves. Each man creates his own time of destruction. Each time a man does not use the seed that is within him in the proper manner and instead uses it in a destructive manner, then that is his time of destruction. The way in which a man completes his life determines his *qiyāmah*. His death is his *qiyāmah*.

People talk about some other Day of Reckoning, *Qiyāmah*. They have been saying that for the last fifty million years. It is not like that. Births and deaths have been going on and on all that time. Man's day of reckoning is at the end of his own life. That is the day when the questions will be asked and accounts will be taken. The day each individual dies is his own day of reckoning. He will be questioned and then depending on the answers, the appropriate punishment will be decided.

Qiyāmah is a word used commonly in everyday speech. The Qur'an mentions the word *qiyāmah*, or the day of *qiyāmah*, and people could interpret it in many ways. However, when the Prophet Muhammad ﷺ was asked, "When will we meet you again?" he replied, "You can meet me near the bridge called *Sirātul-Mustaqīm*, the Straight Path; you can meet me at the foot of the scale of justice. This is the scale that weighs good and evil. I will stand at the foot of this scale, at the spot where good and evil are weighed. This is where your *qiyāmah* will take place, and you can see me there. When you are able to distinguish between right and wrong, taking only what is right, you will see me at this place, the place from which you understand the difference between good and evil and separate them." This is what it means.

Your good and evil are not weighed at some distant place where you go after you die. You, yourself, must use your wisdom to separate right from wrong, and at this place where you weigh good and evil with wisdom, you will see the truth. That truth is the scale. It is the *Rasūl* ☾. The *Rasūl* ☾, the truth, is the pointer on the scale. That is why he said he could be seen there.

When the Prophet ☾ was about to leave the world, to be transformed, his followers asked him, "When will the world end?" He answered by raising one finger. People interpreted this in various ways. Some said it meant one crore, or ten million years. Others said it meant one *yuga*, or fifty million years. Some said it was one *lakh*, or one hundred thousand years. Some said it was one thousand years, and others said one hundred years. Still others said it meant one month, one week, or one day. But Abū Bakr ☾ said, "Allah is the only One who knows." He raised one finger to show that there is only One who knows—that One is Allah. All the calculations the others had made up until that time were brushed away, and the explanation based on 'the One' was accepted.

Similarly, the meanings and explanations of the chapters (*sūrats*) in the Qur'an that were sent down from the wealth of Allah (*daulat*) can be known only by one who has that same wealth. Only he can understand their true meaning. Others will interpret the meanings in various ways, and they will therefore interpret *qiyāmah* in many ways, but it is only when they reach that place of truth and look, that they will know.

The hell we have to cross over is full of fire, the fire of our base desires (*nafs*), the fire of our cravings. Only when we walk over the fire, over the vilest of canals, the birth canal, will we see the scale of judgment on the other shore. This is what they say. If I had gone there and seen it, I would know and I could tell you about it. But, I have not gone there yet, so I can only repeat what has been said.

I have already described hell in *The Ten Mystical Experiences*.[1] How can I tell you what it is like? I did see hell with my own eyes. When I was flying over, I could see each one of the seven hells. Finally, I saw the fire of hell. I also saw the different beings that had fallen into hell. They no longer looked like human beings but had the appearance of dogs and various other animals, with their tongues and noses either missing or crushed. I saw all this with my own eyes, as I flew over all seven hells. Even now, when I think of it, I shudder with fear.

There is such a thing called hell. However, it is the hell that exists within us that God shows us on the outside. If we have overcome it here, then we will overcome it there. Those who have not overcome it here in this world cannot overcome it there. There is no hell there that is not present here. Only God can save us.

In hell there is a huge roller, like the ones used to flatten stones on paved roads. This roller is two hundred and fifty miles long and the beam by which it is dragged is also the same length. Someone stands next to the beam with a fairly long whip in his hand and forces the people to lie on the ground, like stones strewn on a path. Two hundred to

---

1. In the 1950's, Bawa Muhaiyaddeen related *The Ten Mystical Experiences* which have yet to be published.

two hundred and fifty other people are chained to the beam and are forced to pull the roller over the people lying on the ground. As they pull, they are whipped. They are screaming, and the people being crushed are also howling and wailing. Blood flows everywhere. This goes on from morning until night. Then all those who were crushed take form again and are made to lie down and be crushed once more. Then they are heaped onto a fire burning as high as a mountain. I have seen this.

I saw different people there: a man who butchered goats, a man who butchered cattle, and a man who weighed and sold the flesh of animals. I asked them what they had done, and they told me. I saw all this with my own eyes, and I related some of it in *The Ten Mystical Experiences.* I have had two hundred thousand such experiences, but only ten have been recorded. I have forgotten many of them because so much time has passed.

July 26, 1977

11

CAN ONE ESCAPE FROM HELL AND REBIRTH?

———————————◦⟨∞⟩◦··———————————

Question: You have said that some people go to hell. Once a person goes to hell, can he escape or be released from there?

Bawa Muhaiyaddeen: If we can escape from hell while we are here in this world, then we will have released ourselves from that hell. But if we cannot free ourselves here, how can we be freed there? If we can free ourselves even a little from this worldly hell, we will be freed from that hell.

Question: Bawa, suppose one happens to go to hell, can one escape after that? In other words, does one get another chance to escape from hell?

Bawa Muhaiyaddeen: The point is, my little brother, why are you going to hell?

Questioner: Well, in case I slip up or make a mistake.

Bawa Muhaiyaddeen: If you make a mistake? Consider a gold sovereign. The coin is stamped with a symbol which denotes its purity and value. No one can dispute that. It is pure gold and is worth a great deal. It can be sold for one hundred and forty rupees.

Now, if you take this coin to a goldsmith, he might say, "Well, if you melt this down and make it into a piece of jewelry, it will be much nicer." But to do this, he has to add a little copper to make it malleable. Then he will say, "I must beat the gold and make the ornament hollow. Then I will have to fill the hollow with some lac, or red gum. Afterwards,

107

I will flatten it, shape it, and stretch it. Four or five units of gold dust will be lost in the process. So in order for the ornament to weigh the same as the original gold coin did, I will have to add a little more copper and lac, but when I'm finished, you will have a very beautiful piece of jewelry."

However, because some lac and copper have now been mixed into the gold, it has lost its status of being pure gold. Although it is a beautiful ornament, it can no longer be said to be pure. It has changed.

Similarly, it has been said, "If we miss our opportunity in this life, when will we get another chance? If we miss our opportunity in this birth, when will we get another birth, O Lord?" This is the human birth, in which we have divine analytic wisdom, the sixth state of consciousness (pahuth arivu). This wisdom enables us to discriminate between what is right and what is wrong. It has been said, "To be born as a human being with wisdom is an exalted and rare state. To be born as a male is even more rare. And to be born with eyes that see well and ears that hear well is even more rare. It is still rarer to be born a human being with divine qualities (manu-Īsan). Even more rare is to be born as a wise person, rarer still is to be born as an illumined poet, and rarer than that is to be born as a king. Rarest of all is to be born as a perfected human being (insān kāmil), a true wise man (gnāni)."

If a human life dies and is reborn, even once, its value decreases. The sixth level of consciousness and the ability to discriminate is reduced, and in the next birth one will have five levels of consciousness. There are some learned people who only have these five levels. They have studied the religious texts (purānas), and they have Bachelor's or Master's degrees. But even though they have studied so much, they cannot discriminate between what is wrong and what is right. They do not distinguish between what is permissible and impermissible (halāl and harām) or what is good and evil (*khair* and *sharr*). They have not learned to treat other lives as their own. Nor have they understood through their awareness (*unarchi*) that all lives are one life, that all lives belong to one family, and that all children are of the same family.

These learned people have studied a lot with their five levels of consciousness, but what do they have? They have the powers of earth and have learned about the earth's four hundred trillion, ten thousand energies. They have also studied about the powers of the air and the powers of the base desires (*nafs*) that exist within it. They have studied about creation and the powers of water. They have the fire of anger, arrogance, pride, vengeance, and jealousy. They have held on to the glitters and colors of the moon, the sun, the religions, and the races. These are what they have understood with the five levels of consciousness, so these are the energies (*shaktis*) that work for them.

They do not have the divine analytic wisdom which would enable them to discern and discriminate and realize that there is nothing other than God. They do not realize that God is beyond birth, death, destruction, and appearance, that He lacks nothing and has no form, that He is the only One, the One Treasure that exists within forever. They do not realize any of this. They do not have the wisdom that analyzes and explains. However much you may preach to such a person, however much you may teach him, his heart is locked. He does not have the wisdom that can discern and absorb. Like an echo, the sound goes toward him and returns without entering him. The words return without being absorbed, because he is lacking divine analytic wisdom. Even if he is in hell, he does not see it for what it is; he can only perceive it in accordance with his fifth level of wisdom.

Thus, if one misses the opportunity to realize God in this birth and dies, he will be reborn with only five levels of consciousness. But even so, he must try and make the most of that. Then he will at least receive a station deserving of that level. He will be born seven times with five levels of consciousness and a human face. On the outside he will have a human form, but if you look within you will see a different form. Different powers will be operating within, and if a person misses this opportunity as well, he will be reborn with only four levels of consciousness. If he works hard here, he might at least attain the position given to those at that level. He could at least strive for that. He will be born seven times at this fourth level, and if he does not achieve the maximum attainment of that level, he will be reborn with only three levels of consciousness. He will be born seven times at this level, and if he does not live up to that state, then he will be born with only two levels of consciousness. After that, he will be born with only one level of consciousness. In that birth, he should at least attain the position given to one who is at the first level of consciousness. If he does, then he will be born as either a tree, shrub, grass, bulb, or flower.

Question: Bawa, you say he will become a tree, shrub, grass, or flower. Does that mean that consciousness is increasing?

Bawa Muhaiyaddeen: No, it is decreasing; wisdom decreases.

Question: Will he finally become stone?

Bawa Muhaiyaddeen: No, he doesn't become coal; he becomes a worm. He becomes a worm and goes to hell. Hell is where worms live.

Question: But Bawa, does he never get released from hell?

Bawa Muhaiyaddeen: Released? Freedom? Hell is comfortable for a worm, so he is free there. That is his release. He needs hell. The worm will want for nothing there. It has attained the place where worms live. Therefore, it is freedom for a worm to go and live there. It is a worm's place. It will go to hell and eat whatever comes there.

Question: Can one come back from being a worm?

Bawa Muhaiyaddeen: No, it has lost its opportunity.

Question: Then why should one try if one is going to go to a particular place anyway?

Bawa Muhaiyaddeen: Now, you know that it is hell. It is a place for worms. You cannot get rice in hell; you get a different food there. As soon as you go below, it is hell.

Question: Can this happen to both males and females? Isn't the male reborn in female form?

Bawa Muhaiyaddeen: The questioner is referring to an ancient Tamil song he heard. But who is the female and who is the male? Everyone is female. Only One is male. That is God. Everyone loves Him. He is the only male. We are all female, are we not? It is not this human form that denotes male and female. The song was referring to the soul and God. The soul is the light. It belongs to God and worships God. The soul is neither male nor female. It does not have form. It does not have semen. It does not have lust. It does not have anger. It has no hunger, disease, birth, or death. It has no differences of the 'I' and the 'you'. It has none of these; it is in the same state as God. It is this ray, the soul, that attains God. The rest is just the five elements of earth, fire, water, air, and ether. It is all illusion, it is all *māyā* or lust. A male and a female build a house, live in it, and create the world. That is the cooperative store where mind and desire dwell. Let us leave that behind and return to the place we came from.

Questioner: Bawa, you said when we are born we are like a pure gold sovereign. Then as we grow up, we make some mistakes and we are like the gold that has been beaten by the goldsmith and changed.

Bawa Muhaiyaddeen: The point is you should do the work

while you are still here. You should do it in this very life-time.

Question: We can change?

Bawa Muhaiyaddeen: You should change while you are still here.

Translator: Before we die.

Bawa Muhaiyaddeen: Yes, this is it!

Question: After we have gone to the goldsmith can we still change?

Bawa Muhaiyaddeen: You haven't been to the goldsmith yet! Change yourself now! If you make a mistake, if you hit someone, say, "My God, I have hit him. Please forgive me. I should never do that again. Please accept me." As soon as you realize you have done something wrong you must pray to God for forgiveness and never repeat the same mistake.

You should search for God now. For whatever you say with each breath, you should ask for forgiveness in the next breath. Then it will be pushed away.

Question: What about the goldsmith?

Bawa Muhaiyaddeen: That comes later, if you have missed your opportunity in this birth and are reborn. But you should do the work now. The questions that are asked now, you have to answer now. You have to write the exam now. You have to pass the exam now.

Question: What happens if we pass the test?

Bawa Muhaiyaddeen: You become man-God, God-man.

Question: But isn't it very difficult to do this in one birth?

Bawa Muhaiyaddeen: This is where you should search. That treasure can be found only in this birth. That house exists only in this birth. If you miss the opportunity in this birth, you may have six more lives, but only your face will be of human form. The rest of you will be like a monkey or a donkey. It is only in this birth that you are a true human being (*manu-Īsan*). If you miss this birth, then you are born according to the astrological signs. Those signs are the ram (Aries), bow and arrow (Sagittarius), balance (Libra), virgin (Virgo), scorpion (Scorpio), lion (Leo), or bull (Taurus). But astrology does not apply to a true human being.

Question: Bawa, are you saying that you know who is at what level, that you know who has come back with six levels of consciousness, five levels, four levels, and so forth? Do you know who each one is? Can we know this?

Bawa Muhaiyaddeen: For this you need those eyes and that wisdom; you need the eye of wisdom. Now, I know. When you pass by me and I look within you, I may see something with four legs, I may see a snake, I may see a lion, a tiger, a demon, a cow, a horse, a donkey, or a crab. When I look inside, I will know this. I see this.

May 4, 1974

12

WHAT IS REBIRTH?

————•◦∞◦•————

Questioner: Bawa has said that if we do not make it in this life, in our first birth, then we will be reborn. And as far as I understand the Islamic scriptures, we die, we go to the grave, we are questioned there, and we wait until the final Day of Judgment when the trumpet is blown. So when is it decided upon that we have to go back to the world and be reborn with lower and lower levels of wisdom, until we finally end up in hell as a worm?

Bawa Muhaiyaddeen: Yes, I have talked about this a lot. This is one thing you have to understand. It is while you are living in the world, in this very birth, that you undergo all these rebirths—about 105 million rebirths. Every day, you are being reborn. Every new quality is indeed a rebirth. Every new action is a rebirth. You undergo all these births in this very lifetime.

Look at a person's face, for example. Sometimes his face is a very angry face, like a tiger's. At another time it is like the dark face of satan. At yet another time a face that is broad and open suddenly becomes contracted and pinched. So many faces develop and appear within the one face. The heart and the face reveal the person's state, whether it be happiness, sorrow, anger, vengeance, and all the other states that a person experiences. Each of these is a form that the person has taken at a particular time. In this way, without his even being aware of it, the person is reborn in different forms within his lifetime. This happens all the time, whether

115

he is sleeping or awake, whether he is thinking or dreaming.

Every action performed in this birth is either good or evil, right or wrong. When we go to our grave, we will be questioned, and an account of our actions will be taken. Those who did good will receive what is good and those who did evil will receive their punishment. Each person will receive what he has earned.

On the Day of Questioning (*Qiyāmah*), the trumpet will be blown by Isrāfīl ☉, the angel of air, and everyone will be woken up. When that air is blown by Isrāfīl ☉, the person will rise up in the specific form that he has been reborn in according to the changes in his qualities and actions in this world. It is only then that this new form is revealed. He may have the form of a dog, a cat, or a rat, or some other being, and it is in this form that he will finally be asked the questions and have to account for his actions.

What is this final questioning? It is an account of everything we take with us. What is heaven? Heaven is what we take with us. What is goodness? Goodness is what we take with us. For every small act of goodness that we take with us, one thousand or even ten thousand beautiful things will be spread out before us there. A single good act is made into so many thousands of acts of goodness. Whatever we have done in this world, good or bad, is magnified and stored for us. Heaven is the place where all our good actions and good thoughts have been multiplied thousands and tens of thousands of times and reserved for us.

Precious child, what is the meaning of the saying, "We must die before death?" It means that we must make all the evil qualities, all the qualities of satan within us, die before our death. If those qualities die, then the world within us dies. And if the world within us dies, then all the sins, ghosts, demons, and satans contained within it also die. The desires for earth, gold, and sexual pleasures all die along with the world within us. All that is left is Allah and His power (qudrat). If all the evil qualities die within us, then we die before death and only Allah's qualities, actions, and conduct will remain. Then there will be no death for us. We will have attained eternal life (hayāt). If we attain eternal life, where will we live? We will live in heaven, in God's kingdom.

This is how it is, my child. When that day comes, such a person will no longer be in the grave. He will be in heaven, because any place he is will be heaven. He has no death. Wherever he lives, it will be a palace. On the earth he lives in a palace, and in heaven he lives in a palace. When he is buried, he is in a palace. He has a palace on the outside and one on the inside.

There is a saying by Tamil wise men (gnānis), "If I fail in this birth, O God, when will I ever get another chance?" The explanation of this saying is as follows: This birth is our only birth as a human being with divine analytic wisdom (pahuth arivu). And if we do not succeed in our quest this time, when will we ever obtain such a birth again? Never. If we don't learn what we have come here to learn, we will be subject to many rebirths. Our qualities and wisdom will change. Our actions will change. Our form will change. This is our only birth as a human being, and if we do not change and attain the state of eternal life by dying before death, then we will not obtain God's grace. But if we miss our opportunity in this birth, then all the qualities within divine analytic wisdom will leave us, and all the animal, demonic, and satanic qualities will enter us. We will be subject to anger, hastiness, and hatred, and we will undergo many difficulties. The qualities of jealousy and vengeance and the divisive qualities of 'I and you', 'my religion and your religion' will take hold and lead us to some other place. They will change us. That is why it is said that if we miss our chance in this birth, we will have given up our human form and be subject to many different forms and many different births. This is what the wise men were talking about.

If a man becomes a true human being (*insān*), then there is only one birth. If all his qualities die and the world within him dies before physical death comes to overtake him, then he will die within Allah and be absorbed into His qualities. That is the meaning of this saying. Do you understand, my child? I give you my love.

May 3, 1985

13

CREMATION AND THE DEBT WE OWE
TO THE EARTH

————————◦∞◦————————

Question: Why does the Bawa Muhaiyaddeen Fellowship want to establish a cemetery and have the body buried, rather than having it cremated?

Bawa Muhaiyaddeen: God has said that in the primal beginning (*āthi*) the earth was extremely valuable; everything was contained within it. I have given many explanations about this.

At the time of the primal beginning God had not yet created man. He had created earth, fire, water, air, and ether, each with their own inherent value. Because of this, each element became proud. Even though God had created them, each element vainly boasted, "I am the greatest! Nothing can be compared to me!"

Then God said, "I must join these five elements together to take away their vanity, and I will use the light of the *Nūr Muhammad*[1] to do this. I will create all lives using equal portions of these five elements, bringing them to a state of unity and destroying their pride."

Having created the jinns, the fairies, the heavenly beings, the earth, the sky, and so on, God then brought forth the light of *Nūr Muhammad* from within Himself. God

————————————————

1. *Nūr Muhammad*—The beauty of the qualities and actions of the powers (*wilāyāt*) of Allah, the radiance of Allah's essence (*dhāt*) which shines with the resplendence of His truth. See glossary.

asked His creations, "Who will accept this light? If anyone is able to accept this, please come forward." When the other lights looked at the brilliance of *Nūr Muhammad*, they became absorbed within it.

God again asked, "Who will come forward to accept this?" They all replied, "O Creator, *Yā Rahmān*, O God, this light has absorbed all the other lights; therefore, how can any of us receive it?"

Yet again God asked, "Is there anyone who can carry and accept My *Nūr Muhammad*?"

Then the earth humbly came forward saying, "I will accept this light."

"O earth, you have brought ruin upon yourself," resonated the sound of God. "You have created your own downfall. This light is pure, while you contain colors, dirt, refuse, creatures, and many other diverse things. Everything grows within you, so how can you accept what is pure? O earth, I will give you this light, this trust. It belongs to Me. You have hastily accepted this, and by doing so you have brought about your own destruction. Now you must consider how you can return this light to Me in the same condition. I am giving it to you, and it must be returned without any flaw or imperfection."

And God said, "These five elements are the things I created first. I will combine them within all created lives. They will be common to all lives, and they will provide the basis and support for the bodies of all lives. But first, I have to make them united. I must destroy their pride." In order to create this unity God brought forth the light known as *Nūr Muhammad* from within Himself and instructed this light to go to each element and make it recite the *kalimah*—*Lā ilāha ill-Allāhu Muhammadur-Rasūlullāh.* There is nothing other than You, O God. Only You are God, and Muhammad is the Messenger of God.

Nūr Muhammad, resplending with light, proceeded to obey God's command. First *Nūr Muhammad* saw the element of fire and greeted it, saying, "*As-salāmu 'alaikum*, may the peace of God be upon you, O fire! What life-force do you contain?"

Fire boasted, "Nothing is greater than I! Nothing is more clever than I! I am more powerful than anything else in the world. I am the greatest and nothing can be compared to me!"

Nūr Muhammad responded gently, "O fire, water can humble and subdue you. When you intend to destroy something, air can move you away from that particular place. Earth can suffocate you with its dust. Many things can subdue you. Therefore, how can you say you are greater than anything else? There are things which are greater than you. So what is the basis for your boasting?

"Besides this, O fire, there is the One who has created you and all lives. He is God, your Creator. While you are claiming you can do everything, you have not thought about this One and considered His true worth. In reality, you are the lowest of all creations. Yours is the least of all powers. Have you not reflected on this?"

Fire conceded, "What you say is true. O light, what life-force do you have?"

"I have no force," *Nūr Muhammad* humbly replied. "I have no power or strength. I am a slave to the All-Powerful One, I am the lowest of all lives, and I am intermingled within them all. The One God who created me is the only One with power. I acknowledge Him as the Almighty One, and I am His slave. O fire, intend His name, focus on Him, trust Him, and have absolute faith (*īmān*) in Him. He will protect you. Everything is in His hands."

And fire said, "You have spoken the truth."

Then, so that unity and compassion would be understood by fire when it was within all lives, *Nūr Muhammad* instructed it to accept and recite the *kalimah*. "*Lā ilāha ill-Allāhu Muhammadur-Rasūlullāh*. There is nothing other than You, O God. Only You are God and Muhammad is the Messenger of God," fire declared without hesitation.

Next *Nūr Muhammad* saw water and greeted it, saying, "*As-salāmu 'alaikum*, may the peace of God be with you, O water. What life-force is contained within you?"

Water boasted haughtily, "I am truly great! Nothing is greater than I. I can destroy and control anything I want—forests, lands, mountains, and shores. I can make ocean into land and land into ocean. I can make cities disappear and destroy the entire world. Really, I can do everything! Nothing is comparable to me."

"O water," chided *Nūr Muhammad* gently, "there are things greater than you. Air can make you change your direction and push you here and there. Rocks and mountains have been placed to make you yield and subdue your force as you flow along. Furthermore, all lives will use you for both good and bad purposes. Some will drink you, some will wash themselves with you, and others will deposit feces and filth in you and pollute you. You will also be trapped in ponds and lakes which become putrid and foul. Worms, maggots, and many other disgusting things will live and grow within you. You will be made to lose your clarity and become repulsive, slimy, and impure and develop a foul odor. Human beings will confine and trap you in many ways by constructing pools and reservoirs. Endless numbers of creatures will grow within you, and all lives will use you to cleanse themselves. This being so, what is the basis for your boasting and arrogance? There are many things more powerful than you!"

Water inquired, "O *Nūr Muhammad*, what power have you?"

"I have no power. Only Allah is powerful," replied the

Nūr. "He is omnipotent. With strength He created everything, all energies and all lives. He protects everything, and He controls and rules over everything. He is mighty and great, and I am merely His slave. I have no power. I am one who serves all lives according to His commandment. I believe in Him. Allah, the Lone One who rules and sustains, is the only powerful One. I have absolute faith in Him, I am surrendered to Him, and I humble myself before Him as my Creator and Protector. O water, believe in Him with certainty, have absolute faith (*īmān*) and bow down to Him."

Nūr Muhammad then instructed the water to recite the *kalimah*, and it did so without hesitation, "*Lā ilāha ill-Allāhu Muhammadur-Rasūlullāh.*"

Next the *Nūr* saw air and greeted it, saying, "*As-salāmu 'alaikum,* may the peace of God be with you, O air. What life-force is contained within you?"

The air boasted, "There is nothing more powerful than I! I contain great power. Nothing can control me and I can do anything I want. I can destroy jungles and smash trees. I am mighty in nature, unconquerable!"

Nūr Muhammad laughed gently and said, "O air, there are countless barriers to control you and obstruct the disasters you perpetrate. Tall mountains and majestic trees can block you and dissipate your force by diffusing you on all four sides. They will stand before you and keep you from proceeding. And above all these, there is your Creator who created earth, fire, water, ether, and you. Have you forgotten Him? If He wished, He could overpower you in a second."

"Well, what power do you have, *Nūr Muhammad?*" asked the air.

"I have no power. All power is with God, my Creator. I am His slave. I accept Him and have placed my faith and certitude in Him. He is exalted and supreme, and you must also place your trust in Him. He will protect you.

"O air, you will look at the faces of the creations and be able to see them, but they will be unable to see you. No one will be able to enjoy your beauty. This is a defect within you. Therefore, how can you say you are great?"

The air accepted this, and *Nūr Muhammad* instructed it to recite the *kalimah*. "*Lā ilāha ill-Allāhu Muhammadur-Rasūlullāh*," it declared without hesitation.

Then *Nūr Muhammad* greeted ether, "*As-salāmu 'alaikum*, may the peace of God be with you, O ether. What life-force is within you?"

Ether claimed, "I am greatest of all. I have so many beautiful lights and colors. Nothing can be compared to me!"

"There is One who is greater than you," explained *Nūr Muhammad*. "He has countless powers. He has many acids that can kill you in all the seven worlds. And He has many different colors. Allah is the only One who is great!" *Nūr Muhammad* then instructed ether to recite the *kalimah*, "*Lā ilāha ill-Allāhu Muhammadur-Rasūlullāh*," and ether obeyed.

Finally, *Nūr Muhammad* saw the earth and said, "*As-salāmu 'alaikum*, O earth. What life-force is within you?"

The earth answered humbly, "O *Nūr Muhammad*, I have no force, I have no strength or power. Allah alone is the Mighty One. He is the greatest and I have no greatness. All lives will trample me, stamp on me, spit on me, and degrade me. They will dig me up and carry me from place to place. Despicable and hellish things, such as corpses and waste products, will be buried within me. I will have to endure all this. Therefore, I am the lowest of all lives. I believe in God alone."

Upon hearing this the light of *Nūr Muhammad* said, "You are truly the greatest of all these!" The *Nūr* joyfully embraced and kissed the earth.

Then this light of *Nūr Muhammad* said, "O earth, God will create all lives out of you and they will grow within you.

Gold, water, fire, air, ether, gems, metals, and all that is valuable will be placed within you. The beautiful qualities of patience, gratitude, and forbearance will also be placed within you. You will be the body and the vital pulse of all lives. God will create everything through you. He will dispense His wealth through you and make lives peaceful. God is offering you this precious gift. You are to be the mother of creation, the patient mother to all lives, the wealth to God's creations." The earth kissed the light back and when they embraced, the light of *Nūr Muhammad* entered into the earth.

That is why today, when we prostrate in prayer, we press our forehead on the earth, in acknowledgement of *Nūr Muhammad.* Everyone bows toward the earth. It is used for all our bodily needs. We live on it, we sleep on it, we eat on it, we grow on it, and we benefit from it in many ways. God placed many elemental energies (*shaktis*) and great wealth in the earth.

The earth immediately affirmed the *kalimah,* saying, "*Lā ilāha ill-Allāhu Muhammadur-Rasūlullāh.* There is nothing other than You, only You are God, and Muhammad is the Messenger of God. You, Allah, are glorious and supreme. I believe in You and I place my trust in You. I have absolute faith (*īmān*) in You. I accept Muhammad as Your Messenger, and I accept this light as Your representative, as the *Nūr,* as Your plenitude. I accept this and worship You with absolute faith, certitude, and determination."

Some time later, God decided to create all lives. Then, taking one fistful of earth, fire, water, air, and ether, He created the body of all living things. Then He decided to create man. But seventy thousand years prior to this He had already created man's sustenance (*rizq*)—his food, water, wealth, comforts, warmth, and everything else he would need. When the allotted amount of food, water, fire, air, and

ether for each man is over, he is called back by 'Izrā'īl ⊛,
the Angel of Death. This is called his destiny (nasīb). Man
has this destiny because his sustenance (rizq), his allotted
portion, was created before he came into the world.

After creating all other lives, God set about creating
man, and He intended to make man the most exalted and
wisest of all His creations. He gave three states of consciousness (feeling, awareness, and intellect) to all other lives, but
to man He gave four additional levels of consciousness:
judgment, subtle wisdom, divine analytic wisdom, and divine
luminous wisdom. These were given to man so that he could
be the father, the sheikh, the sayyid, the nurturer, and God's
vice-regent to all creations. Man was given the qualities that
would enable him to give comfort and peace to others.

God called for Angel Jibrīl ⊛ and said, "Go to the four
corners, the four directions of the world. Collect earth from
each corner until you have one fistful of earth and bring it
back to me."

Angel Jibrīl ⊛ obeyed. The light of Nūr Muhammad had
already entered earth when the Nūr kissed it, and the earth
had acquired divine wisdom. So when Angel Jibrīl ⊛ was
collecting the earth, it cried out, "O Jibrīl do not take earth
from me. In the name of God, do not take earth from me. All
beings that God creates through me will go in the direction
of hell. They will sin, cause harm, and destroy others. They
will lie, cheat, murder, and live in an impermissible (harām)
way. They will not realize the truth. They will grow wealthy
through me and forget God who is my Master, and therefore, they will go to hell. If the children created through me
go to hell, I will be unable to bear it. It will cause me untold
grief and eternal sadness if my children end up in hell.
Therefore, I beg of you, please, in the name of God, do not
take earth from me!"

Upon hearing this, Jibrīl ⊛ dropped the earth and

returned to God, telling Him everything that had transpired. Then God sent Angel Mīkā'īl ⓔ to collect the earth. The same thing happened and Mīkā'īl ⓔ returned to God. Then Angel Isrāfīl ⓔ was sent down, but he also returned in the same manner.

Finally God sent the Angel of Death, 'Izrā'īl ⓔ. When 'Izrā'īl ⓔ was collecting the earth from the four corners of the world, earth appealed to him, saying, "In the name of God, I implore you, do not take earth from me!"

But 'Izrā'īl ⓔ responded, "Complain to the One on whom you made this oath! He is the very One who commanded me to bring this to Him. Make your appeal to Him!" and he gathered one fistful of earth from the four corners and took it to God.

Then the voice of God was heard to say, "Now take this fistful of earth to *Karbalā'*, the central point of the world." 'Izrā'īl ⓔ went and deposited the earth there.

The world says that *Karbalā'*, the central spot, is between Jerusalem and Jiddah. They say that Adam ⓔ was created there, but there is another meaning to this. That one fistful of earth, that *Karbalā'*, is also the inner heart of man, and within it God kept the eighteen thousand universes and the fifteen realms.[2] He placed all these things within the mystery (*sirr*) of man. This is man's battlefield, his heart— this one fistful of earth.

As this one fistful was being taken from the earth, God said, "O earth, what you say is true. I did create you, and I

2. Bawa Muhaiyaddeen often talks of the fifteen realms and the fourteen spheres within the form of man. The fifteenth is the heart in the center, the focal point for man. Above that there are seven worlds and below there are seven worlds. Explanations of this concept can be found in *The Guidebook to the True Secret of the Heart*, Vol. 2 pp. 123-138 and in *The Wisdom of the Divine*, Vol. 3 p. 21, both by Bawa Muhaiyaddeen.

will create many things through you. I will also create laws and a destined limit (*nasīb*) for each thing. In the proper manner, I will create the body, the life, and the necessary food and nourishment for each being that I create out of you. I alone will be the Judge. *Bismillāhir-Rahmānir-Rahīm*—for that fistful of earth, I alone will be the Nourisher, Protector, and Sustainer. I will be its Emperor, its Ruler, its *Badushāh*. Just as I was Your Creator and Lord, I will be the Lord, the *Rabb*, for the one whom I am going to create through you, and I alone will be the Protector.

"O earth, I am telling you that I am responsible for creation, protection, nourishment, and for giving peace to My creations. I will be the Judge, I will make the final decision, and I will be responsible for the day of reckoning and for life in the hereafter. You are not responsible for this. Therefore, it is not necessary for you to carry that burden. I will place the destiny within each life, and according to that destiny and agreement there will be certain restrictions and a day of death according to those restrictions. After death there will be a judgment for that life. There will be a day of reckoning, a day of questioning, and a decision. For the results of that questioning, I will create a heaven and a hell.

"It is I who will place within each man both what is permissible and impermissible (*halāl* and *harām*), good and bad (*khair* and *sharr*), and the secret and the manifestation (*sirr* and *sifāt*). I am the One who gives him these things, and I am the One who judges him in the end. I will give the appropriate kingdom to each, according to the manner in which he conducts himself. If a man conducts himself in a good way, he will be given My kingdom of heaven. If he does not conduct himself properly, he will be given My kingdom of hell. I am the Ruler of both heaven and hell. I am the Monarch of all three worlds—the world of the souls, this world, and the hereafter. You are not responsible for this, O earth, and you need not worry or feel sad about it. It was I who created you and gave you great power, glory, and wealth. It is also I who will distribute this wealth. It is not your responsibility.

"However, the one fistful of earth that I take from you will be on loan. That earth belongs to you. It was given to you. The lives that I create will be created from you and will also obtain their nourishment from you and live and grow on you. I will use you to form their bodies. They will drink your water, utilize your fire and your air, and eat things that grow out of you. This is the 'common wealth' that I have given to you. I have given you earth, fire, water, air, and ether to be used in common by all My creations. I will create all beings in this way, and you must remain available and of common use to all.

"All beings, even birds and animals, will have a connection to these five elements. Whoever is able to cut these connections and understand Me while he is growing and developing, whoever does this and bows in obeisance to Me, I will bow in obeisance to him. Whoever loves Me, I will love him. Whoever takes one step toward Me, searching for Me, I will take ten steps toward him. Whoever calls out to Me once, I will call out ten times to him. Whoever prostrates once to Me, I will prostrate ten times to him. Whoever praises Me once, I will praise him ten times.

"An infinite number of mouths, ears, eyes, noses, and hands are contained within Me. With these ears I will hear him, with these eyes I will see him, with these mouths I will communicate with him, and with these hands I will embrace him. This is My wealth (rahmat). Therefore, O earth, do not grieve. This is why I have created what is known as destiny and why I have placed a limit, an agreement, on all lives. I will call each life back according to that agreement.

"O earth, from that one fistful of earth taken on loan

from you, I will increase man by one thousand fistfuls, and I will also make him return those thousand fistfuls to you. This is My debt, the obligation I will fulfill. When man's agreement is over, I will repay that debt to you. I take this fistful of earth in trust from you, and if any man does not repay this, it will become his primary debt on Judgment Day. He will be punished. I will return each man to the same exact place from which the fistful of earth was taken to create him. I will place each body in the appropriate spot and seize the soul. I will do this according to each individual's limit or agreement. Therefore, O earth, do not concern yourself any further about this matter. It is for this reason that I told 'Izrā'īl to place the one fistful of earth in the central place or *Karbalā'*. This is the heart and within it is the secret. You need not worry about it."

God kept the portion of earth in this place for seventy thousand years, after which He made it rain for seven years in order to make it luxuriant. Then He took the earth and created the form of Adam ﷺ. Next, because the earth and *Nūr* had embraced, God impressed the light of *Nūr Muhammad* on Adam's ﷺ forehead. That spot is known as the eye of wisdom, the *kursī*. Even if our physical eyes are closed, if we open the other eye we can see through that eye of God's grace, the eye of divine wisdom and knowledge (*gnānam* and *'ilm*). One who is in this state has a beautiful form. This is why he is known as *Sūratul-Insān*, *Sūratul-Qur'ān*, or *Sūratul-Fātihah*.

At the time God was creating Adam ﷺ, satan existed in heaven as the leader of the jinns. He was called Abū, and he came with one thousand of his followers to see what was happening. When satan looked at Adam ﷺ, he saw how incredibly beautiful he was. Because that light was within Adam ﷺ, he was very beautiful and resplendent.

Adam's ﷺ gaze appeared to look intently at satan.

Satan said haughtily, "O Adam, are you the man that God created? You are made out of mere earth, yet you stare at me like that? Your gaze makes me afraid! If God places you beneath me, under my control, I will help you in any way I can, but I warn you, if He places you above me, I will do many terrible things to torment you."

Then the face that was resplendent with light blossomed and gazed even more piercingly at Abū, and satan said scornfully, "You dare to stare at me in this manner while you are still made of earth." Satan spat at Adam (☮), and as soon as the spittle fell on Adam's (☮) belly, its poison entered his body. That spittle became the afterbirth.

Seeing this God said, "O Jibrīl, go quickly to Adam. Satan has spat on My pure creation. His evil venom of jealousy, pride, and envy has entered My Adam and polluted him. Go quickly and remove it!" Jibrīl (☮) went at once and with two fingers he pinched out that piece of earth where the spittle had landed. That spot became man's navel, and this is why that place is slightly indented. It has become one of the twenty-eight letters which make up the human body.[3]

That one letter which was pinched out of Adam (☮) was given to the dog. It was placed on the crown of the head of the dog. At the time Adam (☮) received the soul and arose, the dog also arose. Because of that one letter on the dog's head, it is a grateful animal. It can live with man and follow him; it listens to and loves its master. But except for the place on the top of its head, where it cannot lick, the rest of the dog's body is foul, containing desire and all other evil qualities.

God then placed the soul in Adam (☮). It entered through the crown of his head, the 'arsh, and descended downward through the body. The brain began to function

---

3. See footnote 6 on page 24.

but the rest of the body was still earth. It descended to the eyes, and the eyes became lit and could see. Then it descended to the nose, and the nose could smell. It went to the ears, and the ears could hear. It went to the tongue, and Adam ﷺ spoke. Then, even though he was only half-formed, once the soul had entered the chest, Adam ﷺ tried to push himself up with his two hands. "O Adam, have patience." God said, "Look, you are only half-formed; part of your body is in the form of flesh and bone, while the other half is still unformed in earth. Even so, you are hastily trying to get up. This is a sign that man will be an impatient creature. He will surely be hasty!" Then Adam ﷺ sneezed, and the soul descended into the rest of his body.

God then instructed the angels to invite Adam ﷺ to heaven. There God called all the prophets, the illumined beings (olis), and all the heavenly beings, saying, "I am making Adam the leader. Stand behind Adam and pray to Me." They all obeyed except for satan and one thousand of his followers.

Upon seeing this God sternly commanded satan, "O Abū, stand behind Adam and worship Me!"

But satan replied, "O God, I know how to worship You, but I will never worship You standing behind Adam. He is created out of earth and I am created out of fire, therefore I cannot stand behind him."

"Man is praying to Me. Stand behind him and worship Me!" God commanded again.

But satan adamantly refused, "I will never stand behind him."

Once again God ordered, "O detestable one, worship Me standing behind man." Still satan refused.

Finally God cursed satan, saying, "O mal'ūn, O cursed one, who has gone astray! There is no room for you here. I am sending you to hell."

"I am quite prepared to go to hell," satan answered. "Adam is my enemy, and therefore, before I go, I want Your permission to ruin Adam and all of his followers."

"One who follows Me will never follow you, and one who follows you will never follow Me," God answered. "If you intend to spoil one who has submitted himself to Me, you will retreat in disgrace. Your power will diminish. You cannot ruin a follower of Mine without My permission. You do not have the power or ability to lead astray anyone who has surrendered to Me. Now go!"

Satan argued further, "Please give me permission to lose my outer form and creep into man, wherever he is, and to ruin him from within and from without."

"You can only go where there is darkness; you can never go where there is light. If you try to enter someone who lives with faith in Me, you will have to withdraw in disgrace. Get out, satan!"

But satan still persisted, "No matter how much I fail, I will keep trying. Even to man's last moment on earth, I will do my utmost to make him a victim of my fire so that he will be unable to repay his debt to You. If I can't do anything else, I will make him do this!"

"O despicable one," God's sound thundered, "whoever follows Me will live his life as earth and give his life back as earth, but whoever follows you and lives his life in fire will end his life in fire and will never pay back his debt to the earth. Whoever enjoys your riches of darkness and torpor and acquires your qualities of anger, envy, jealousy, attachment, backbiting, prejudice, arrogance, *karma*, illusion, falsehood, deceit, pride, revenge, and whoever believes in your wealth and advertisements for hell will be in the fire of hell. Even while in the physical body, his life will burn in fire. He will live in great sorrow and finally end up in your fire. But if he lives with Me, if he intends Me and practices

My qualities of patience, contentment, trust in God, and giving all praise to God,[5] if he treats all lives as his own life, helping and giving peace to other lives, and if he keeps My three thousand gracious qualities within him and bestows compassion on all lives, he will rule My kingdom. But one who possesses your property and your qualities will forever be a victim to fire. Both while he is living and when he dies, he will be consumed by fire. Now get out satan!"

Satan and his one thousand angels and jinns who were his followers, were then thrown from heaven and landed on earth. Even so, satan was still able to travel up through the seven heavens and perform his magic. On earth he had powers which enabled him to speak through statues, rocks, and idols. During the time of Nimrod and Pharaoh, he used these powers and caused so much difficulty to the children of Adam ☺ in Egypt and Jerusalem. God had to send down the prophets, one by one, to reduce the forces of satan, and finally, through Prophet Muhammad ☺, the power to speak through idols was taken away from him.

Satan will forever try to trick us. Even at the final stage of our lives, he will try to have our body cremated so that we will burn in fire and not repay our debt. He will try to burn the entrusted treasure within us. Those who have absolute faith in God will never do this. They know they have to return the debt they owe to the earth. They know that the prophets have instructed them to do so. God said, "I will forgive whoever pays back that final debt, that trust which I owe to earth. But whoever does not pay back that debt will be punished, and I will send him to the fire of hell. They will have many rebirths as dogs and foxes and be subject to hell."

This is what has been said. This is why those who have wisdom and those who have perfect faith in God (*īmān*) were

---

5. *sabūr, shakūr, tawakkul-'alallāh, al-hamdu lillāh*

told by the prophets to bury their dead in the earth. If the
body is buried in the earth, then each of the five elements
will take back its share. Earth will take the portion of earth,
fire will take the portion of fire, water will take the portion
of water, air will take the portion of air, and ether will take
the portion of ether. The debt owed to these five angels will
be repaid.

   This is what has been told to the prophets and to those
with absolute faith (*īmān*). The prophets told man, "Give back
to the earth what belongs to the earth. Repay your debt.
This is very important. Make sure you have a proper burial.
If you give yourself to fire, that fire belongs to satan. It is
better to give your corpse to water than to fire, because the
corpse will at least sink to the bottom of the ocean or lake
and finally be consumed by the earth. When a man dies, he
will weigh one thousand fistfuls of earth. Even an obese man
will be reduced in weight at death, and he, too, will give
those one thousand fistfuls back to the earth. God has
created it to be so.

   My children, this is why people establish cemeteries
and return their bodies to the earth as is their duty. But satan
tries to put them in fire, make them fall off the path, and
keep them from repaying their debt. This is why we talk
about the need for a cemetery.

   We have a vast cemetery within ourselves, the cemetery
of hell. We have buried many things here. This is a cemetery
of fire which we feed continually. We feed the fire of our
base desires and cravings. If we extinguish this fire with the
qualities of patience, contentment, trust in God, and praise
of God[6] then we will realize the truth and satan will not

---

6. *sabūr, shakūr, tawakkul-'alallāh,* and *al-ḥamdu lillāh*

touch us. If we are not deceitful, if we do not steal, lie, take the property of others or trick others, and instead if we maintain a state of patience, then we will extinguish the fire while we are still alive. If this fire is put out, satan will not come near us. He will be unable to throw his fire into our fire. It is said that the Ten Commandments will fly away when hunger overtakes us. If we fuel our fire here, satan will be able to fuel it from afar, and we will be destroyed. In order to feed this fire of hunger, we will have to lie, steal, be hasty, backbite, find fault with others, murder others, and so on. Instead, for each drop of water we receive, we should say, "All praise is to God. *Al-hamdu lillāh,*" knowing that our nourishment *(rizq)* could have been placed in that one drop by God.

Even if we receive only one seed to eat, we should say, "All praise is to God. *Al-hamdu lillāh.*" Even if we get only one tiny leaf to eat, we should be pleased and say, "All praise is to God. *Al-hamdu lillāh.* In the name of God, Most Gracious, and Most Merciful. *Bismillāhir-Rahmānir-Rahīm.*" God may also have kept our nourishment in the air. Whatever we receive for the moment, praise Allah and say, *"Al-hamdu lillāh."* For whatever we are to receive the next moment, say, "I trust only in You, O God. *Tawakkul-'alallāh."* With this perfect faith and certitude, we should extinguish this fire. Then satan cannot cut away our faith, wisdom, or truth. Hell will not come near us. Please think very carefully about this.

The grave we will be buried in is only five or six feet deep, but our stomach is a vast cemetery. If we can overcome this one-span grave within our stomach, then we can overcome that other grave, and we will have endless peace. *Āmīn.* May God bless us with this. May He give us His grace and His peacefulness.

In some countries, everyone helps bury the dead in the proper manner. It is considered an honor and a duty to do this. Four people will dig the grave, others will donate a shroud, perfume, incense, or whatever is needed, and a priest, or *lebbe*, will say the appropriate prayers. Even the poorest man will be buried this way. There is no recognition of whether the person was rich or poor; the only wish is to see that the body is buried correctly.

In Muslim countries, there is no charge for burial nor is a coffin used. People will fight for the honor of donating the shroud. And as the body is carried on a bier to the cemetery, everyone will jostle to carry it. If a corpse is found on the road or in a public place, everyone will help bury that person. This is true Islam. There is no death tax, there is no burial expense, and everyone unites to bury the person.

If this custom existed in all countries, it would be much better. It is really amazing to observe the burial process in some places. There is a charge for the embalming, a charge for the funeral home, a charge for the coffin, a charge for the church, and a charge for the burial. There is even a charge for the minister. The whole thing usually costs four to five thousand dollars. This is truly astonishing! This is satan's work. He has set it up this way so that people will decide to cremate their dead because it is cheaper and easier. Here burial is a big business. Even after you are dead, money has to be paid to take you away. What will happen to the corpse if you don't pay? I don't understand this. This is astonishing. It is the same thing that Pharaoh did in earlier times. Pharaoh made himself wealthy from the money he collected by taxing the dead. This is what some countries are now doing.

That is why I think it necessary for the common good of all to purchase land for our own cemetery. Even so, we find there are many laws and legal implications because everything is a business. Many things are required, even a casket. These are useless laws for man.

Question: Since it is a law to have a coffin, does that prevent the body from being given back to the earth?

Bawa Muhaiyaddeen: It is not good. The earth, the body, must touch the earth. This is the correct way.

Questioner: Not only do they put the body in a casket, but some people erect concrete vaults around it. This is even the law in some states.

Bawa Muhaiyaddeen: This is only in the West. In the East, in places like India and Ceylon, it does not happen that way. Coffins are not required. Burial is in the earth itself.

Question: Well, what can we do?

Bawa Muhaiyaddeen: There may be state laws, but they also permit one to follow the tenets of one's religion. Let us try to work it out peacefully through these laws.

Question: Bawa talks about fire as being of the nature of satan. I want to know if the fire can also have an element of purification. Sometimes I feel the fire burning inside me, and I don't know whether to discharge it immediately or whether it is actually having a purifying effect. (This last sentence was translated as: Sometimes he feels that the fire is giving him peace.)

Bawa Muhaiyaddeen: How can it bring you peace? Fire burns everything to ashes. The temperature today is ninety-two degrees. Does that bring us peace?

Question: But could it be burning up something bad within us?

Bawa Muhaiyaddeen: It will never burn up anything that is bad.

Question: So what do you do when you feel this within you?

Bawa Muhaiyaddeen: Pour some water on it. Pour the grace and wealth of God (*rahmat*) on it. In all situations, pour over it the qualities of patience, contentment, trust in God, and praise of God. Pour those intentions over it, then satan will be subdued.

Question: Could that be done through *dhikr* (the constant remembrance of God)? Is that the best way?

Bawa Muhaiyaddeen: Yes.

August 3, 1980

14

REALIZING GOD BEFORE DEATH; SUICIDE; ACCIDENTS

Question: According to my understanding of Bawa's teachings, he says that God's forgiveness is with us until our last breath, and that after our last breath we are separated from God. Thus, it is important for us to realize God during our lifetime. Is this because there is no reaching God after death?

Bawa Muhaiyaddeen: That is correct. You must realize whatever has to be realized before you die. Everything you have to search for must be sought while you are still alive. If you are able to merge with God while you are alive, you will never be separated from Him. But if you do not develop that state, you will be separated from Him both while you are alive and after you have died. You cannot accomplish this after you leave. You will only face judgment.

Question: Does that mean nothing can be done to help the dead through communication, prayer, or anything else?

Bawa Muhaiyaddeen: Nothing can be done after one dies. People try to help the dead in various ways. According to the various religious customs, food, clothes, or money are distributed to the poor in the name of those who have died. But these things do not help the dead person. He is judged while he is in the grave itself. His judgment is based on what he has done, not on what others do for him. The wife is judged by what she does and the husband is judged by what he does. There is no way to share any of this. Each individual is left with what he himself has earned. I cannot do this for you and you cannot do this on my behalf.

While you are alive you must realize this explanation. This is why you need a truly realized human being, an *insān kāmil*. It is through such a person that you should attain wisdom and good qualities. With these qualities you must search, change yourself, and earn your own rewards.

Question: One reaches God through His qualities, but is there a possibility of half-reaching God?

Bawa Muhaiyaddeen: You do not have to merge with God. If He gives you a place anywhere in His kingdom, that will be sufficient. God has created eight heavens. If, in accordance with your search, you can gain a place anywhere in His kingdom, that will be sufficient for you. To merge with God, one has to become God Himself. That is extremely difficult.

Question: Does that mean that only a perfected man, an *insān kāmil*, dies within God? What happens to the imperfect man?

Bawa Muhaiyaddeen: What happens to each person depends on what the person has searched for. He will be given a place according to what he has achieved during his lifetime. What he gets will depend on his own search. Until a man's last breath, it is possible for him to change and escape. And until man's last breath it is possible for him to be deceived by satan. He can turn toward God or toward satan. Both possibilities exist.

Question: In psychiatry and in mental institutions, we see a lot of people who have attempted suicide. If a person does commit suicide, what happens to him after he dies?

Bawa Muhaiyaddeen: It is one's own craziness that leads a person into a mental institution. Originally, man has no craziness. No one is born crazy. Man becomes crazy as a result of his own thoughts, bad intentions, desires, or attachments. Whatever he craves causes him to become crazy. In different people, craziness is caused by different desires. It can develop into a desire to rule the world, an obsession for women, for men, for wealth, for children, property, possessions, for farmland, for cats, dogs, or other animals. Some people become obsessed with acquiring titles, becoming politicians, or with their business and careers. Some become obsessed with harming, torturing, or killing others. It is because a person thinks such thoughts, that he becomes crazy. Man brings about his own craziness. The very things he searches for can cause him to end up in a mental hospital, and if the craziness becomes extreme, he may even commit suicide. Wanting to commit suicide is a craziness in itself.

Man brings about his own craziness and ends up in a place appropriate to his state. If a man succeeds in killing himself, he will end up in hell. He could then wander like a ghost, a spirit, or a demon, until his allotted time on earth is completed. Just because a man loses his body does not mean he is dead. There is a limit, a destiny for each person. If he dies before his destined time, he will have to wander as a spirit or ghost in the places in which he dwelt while alive— his house, his farm, his workplace. Only when his ordained time comes will the Angel of Death take his life away. Until then he will adopt the particular form of desire that caused him to commit suicide. I have seen this happen in many places. With my own eyes, I have seen not only the people who have committed suicide, but also the form they took afterward.

I will tell you an experience I had. I went to visit someone in a place called Rozella, in Ceylon. I was walking along a winding mountain road at one o'clock in the morning. It was very dark, and there were no lights. Then I saw a car coming along very fast. I jumped to the side of the road as it whizzed by me, and I caught a glimpse of an English couple in the car. Then I saw another car coming from the opposite direction. I saw the two cars collide and roll down to the bottom of the mountain. It looked so real to me. I ran to the edge of the mountain and looked over. I could hear crying from down below and saw in the distance a car wrapped around a tree trunk. I climbed down the steep precipice, which was dangerously slippery. I had no light and could barely see the car. When I reached the bottom, there was no car, but I could still hear the screaming. I looked up and saw someone standing way up on top of the road, giggling and laughing. So I climbed back up the mountain, with much difficulty. When I got to the top, the person had disappeared. I turned around and saw a woman hanging by her neck from a tree. She was dressed in a nurse's uniform and was giggling very loudly. I saw the couple with her. I caught hold of all three of them, and they told me their story.

They had been living in a house near there during the riots in 1914. The nurse was looking after this couple. Their car collided with a truck driven by some soldiers from a nearby garrison, and everyone died. As they were relating this story, I could see the car collide and then hit the guardrail and both vehicles fall into the river. I looked down the mountain again and saw many, many ghosts. These were the ghosts of the soldiers who had died in other accidents at the same place. They were shouting and howling in a terrible way. I ordered them away from the area, and then they left. Even though they had died in 1914, they were still there when I came by in 1925.

In Ceylon I have captured countless numbers of ghosts and demons, so that they could not harm human beings. Some of these had been conjured up by *mantras* and made to enter people, some were demons which had been created into gods, and others were ghosts of people who had died prematurely. Spirits and ghosts of people who die prematurely are usually found in dark places because they do not like to live where there is light, but ghosts that have been conjured up by *mantras* and witchcraft will go anywhere. This is how they behave.

People who die before their ordained time, whether they die in an accident, commit suicide, or are murdered, will roam in the form of ghosts and demons until their destined time comes. Then they are taken by the Angel of Death to be judged. Those who commit suicide will roam as demons until their day of destiny arrives. This is not God's work. This is the work of someone who kills himself as a result of his own bad habits and crazy thoughts or because of drugs and intoxicants.

October 3, 1980

15

IS IT PERMISSIBLE TO DONATE ORGANS?

————————··◁∞▷··————————

Question: What is the Muslim theory on donating organs? Should we donate our organs to science when we die or is that impermissible, *harām*? Should the body be buried intact?

Bawa Muhaiyaddeen: God did not say anything like that. The Qur'an docs not say any such thing either. Only science tells you to do this.

My child, think of all the sins you have committed. If you donate your eyes, will it all be over? Will you be pardoned? Your eyes have committed many sins on their own. The mind has committed many millions of sins. You cannot donate your organs and be absolved from your sins. On the other hand, you could actually cause harm to the recipient.

You may want to donate something that the earth will eventually consume. I cannot talk about something I do not know. If I did, it would be considered a fault. However, instead of donating your organs after you are dead, it will be better while you are still alive to help all lives as described in the Qur'an. If you help all lives, give charity, and do your duty toward others now, then there will not be anyone who will need your organs after your death.

While we are alive, we are the ones who blind the eyes that can see. We are the ones who ruin the life of a person who is living a good life. It is we who destroy the unity of others. We even try to steal someone else's nourishment (*rizq*). We are the ones who tear apart another life. We break down their houses and drive them away from the land. If we still have the quality of ruining other lives while we are living, what is the use of donating our organs after we are dead?

First, you have to correct your heart and come to rest within God. You must give yourself into the responsibility of God even while you are still alive. If you do not dedicate yourself to God, if you do not surrender to God, what is the use of anything you donate?

The Qur'an does not tell you to donate this or that. It does not tell you to tear open the body, kill it, or cut it up. However, it does tell you to treat the dead body like a flower and bury it in the same manner. The body may have suffered a lot and been hurt while alive, but when it is a corpse, it should be washed and cleaned very gently. The nails and the entire body should be cleansed, softly and with care, and prayers should be recited while this is being done. It is only after it is gently cleansed in this manner that we are told to bury it. It is a very subtle matter. The body to be buried has to be treated like a delicate flower. This is what the Qur'an says. Therefore, you cannot cut up the body and ruin it.

Because of the terrible things that people do in arrogance, many lives are ruined. When man flies in the sky and bombs the ships on the sea destroying many lives, is God responsible for this? No. We cause accidents to happen. When we try to fly beyond God, we get beaten. When one country tries to destroy another, it too will get hurt. When one man tries to attack another, there will be a repercussion.

Nothing has been said in the Qur'an about donating organs. But, according to what God has instituted, nothing belongs to us. Everything was created by Him and everything belongs to Him. When God created Adam ﷺ, He told the earth, "I will take one fistful of earth on loan and create man. I will make him live on the earth, eat from the earth, and increase in size. From his own hand, I will then pay back the loan by returning a thousand fistfuls of earth. This is why a man's body equals one thousand fistfuls of earth when he dies. If at the end of his life he is too big, he will have diarrhea and his body will be purged, reducing it to one thousand handfuls. If he is too small, he will become bloated until he swells to the exact thousand handfuls.

Everything is God's property. Your very life, your body, belongs to Allah. What do you have that belongs to you? What do you have to donate? Perhaps you could donate the clothes you are wearing or the food that you are eating, because they were given to you for the time being. But everything else belongs only to God. Nothing belongs to you. Even your eyes, your mouth, nose, ears, heart, and body, as well as your house, property, and wealth all belong to Allah. You should return them to Him. However, if you want to donate something, it must be done in His name. You must only give charity in the name of Allah, and worship in His name. That will be good. Do everything in the name of Allah.

The only thing that really belongs to you is the good and evil you do. When you die, these are the only two possessions that you will take with you and hand over to God. You should realize that these are the only two things that will determine what you attain tomorrow. Therefore, while you are on this earth, you must try to understand what belongs to you. Understand what is good and what is evil. The mind is like a monkey which jumps from tree to tree. Desire is like a dog which cannot be controlled. Even if you could control the whole world, you cannot control that dog of desire. Even if the whole world diminishes, our mind will not subside. Even if we suppress the world, the demon of the mind will never be suppressed. The monkey mind and the dog of desire are very difficult to control.

If you do find a way to control and subdue the monkey

mind and the dog of desire, then the 'I' will no longer be there. Once the 'I' dies, only God remains. If only God remains, then God will do the work that He must do. If you can attain that state, then it will be good.

Meanwhile, when you are sick, others may help you and you should also help others, but God has not told us to donate organs. This is how it is. In our life sometimes we become entangled. Sometimes we escape and sometimes we cannot.

All praise belongs to God. *Āmīn.*

April 25, 1986

16

Is Death a Grace?

Question: It is said that death is God's grace, or *rahmat*.

Bawa Muhaiyaddeen: Every day is death for man. With every breath we face death. If there is anyone who does not have to face death, he will be Allah.

Allah is the only One who does not die with each breath, with each word, and with each deed. A human being *(insān)* dies with every breath, every word, and every action. He dies repeatedly and wakes up repeatedly. In whatever he does he dies, falls down, and then gets up. That is the state of man. Allah alone does not die; everyone else is dying and being reborn with each breath, word, and action.

Man repeatedly does both good and bad, saying good words and bad words, and therefore he faces judgment every moment. The questions in the grave will never finish for him, and he will have to give the answers repeatedly. His life cannot come to completion, because the questions keep coming, and he must answer. Before he answers each question, death overtakes him, time and time again.

However, if a man can put an end to his dying, the questions and answers will be over, and he will have attained eternal life *(hayāt)*. When a man has eternal life, hell is far removed from him. The one who is eternal is Allah. A person who attains this state will have pushed this world and hell far away from him and will have placed in front of him the power and grace of Allah and the *Rasūl*, Prophet Muhammad ☮. Because of this, he can directly worship the One who is the grace of all the worlds (*Rahmatul-'ālamīn*). This is the state of one who is eternal, but our state is the state of one who is constantly dying.

Up to the final day of our death, we die repeatedly because this is the *rahmat* that Allah has decreed for us. The garland of death is around our neck. Death is wedded to us; it is our wedding garland hung around our neck. However, if we escape from death, we are divorced. The line on our neck is the chain of death, and when we separate ourselves from death, then we are divorced. We have performed *talāq;* we have cut away our connection to this world (*dunyā*) and the hereafter (*ākhirah*).

We must divorce ourselves from three things—earth, gold, and sensual pleasures. That is why in Arabic, one must say three times, "*Talāq, talāq, talāq,* I divorce you, I divorce you, I divorce you." We must free ourselves from our desire for earth, gold, and sensual pleasures and then escape. Otherwise, we have many small deaths, and each time we wake up again. But, if we kill our desires, that will be the great death. If we divorce ourselves from these desires, then we make our own death die. Allah has put all these things to death.

What are the *ahādīth?* What is the Qur'an? When we look carefully and study ourselves, then our own history is the Qur'an. Look at Allah, His creations, and His ninety-nine powers (*wilāyāt*). The entire story of God is within man in the twenty-eight letters. The entire universe (*'ālam*) and the world of the souls (*arwāh*) are within man as the 6,666 verses, embodied in the twenty-eight letters. *Al-hamdu lillāh*—praising God in all situations is also born out of these twenty-eight letters. The praise of God exists only within a true human being (*insān*).

This Qur'an, in the form of man, contains the entire grace of God (*rahmat*). All of everything has been explained within man. Man should look at this Qur'an. God's words and actions are the *abādīth*. Man should look within his inner heart (*qalb*) with wisdom for these *abādīth*. This is what we should understand completely. Man contains the Qur'an within him. Within that are the *abādīth*, and within that are the sounds, resonances, and explanations. Then according to the strength of our faith (*īmān*) and wisdom, we will understand and savor those tastes. The *abādīth* and the Qur'an are within the form of the human being (*insān*). The form of man is the Qur'an and the grace of God (*rabmat*) exists as the *abādīth*. God communicates directly with wisdom saying, "Yā Rasūl." Allah speaks directly with a man of wisdom. This is the *abādīth*.

We should reflect on this. *Al-bamdu lillāh*. All praise is to God.

April 15, 1985

17

ARE HEAVEN AND HELL CREATED THINGS?

Question: Beside the fact that the ultimate is Allah's resplendent light (*Nūr*), are heaven and hell created elements in the hereafter (*ākhirah*), like life is here? One who is promised heaven will get heaven in the hereafter (*ākhirah*) and one who is promised hell will get hell—are those material creations?

Bawa Muhaiyaddeen: Yes, they have been created. When a seed is created, it has an outer covering; that is the part which has to perish. Only the tiny point within the seed germinates and grows. As it grows the rest of the seed is destroyed. The part that is destroyed belongs to hell, while the part that grows has life (*hayāt*). It joins with the essence of Allah (*dhāt*) and has a connection to Him.

Like this, within creation, good (*khair*) and evil (*sharr*) are in Allah's trust (*tawakkul*). In everything that appears, in everything that is created, one portion belongs to the world and will perish, while the other portion belongs to the hereafter (*ākhirah*). A seed is created in this manner, and such is the way of all created things. Everything that has a form contains a portion within it that relates to Allah, to His grace (*rahmat*), and that will never perish. The coverings will perish, and they are *sharr*. One is *khair*, or eternal, the other is *sharr*, or creation, which perishes. One is the essence (*dhāt*). This is the way with all created things.

Question: But the one who is striving for heaven, will he get rivers of milk and meadows of green and gold and things like

155

that? Is heaven like that?

Bawa Muhaiyaddeen: It may be like that, but not in heaven.
The river of milk and the river of honey must flow in his
inner heart (*qalb*). The undiminishing fruit that never perishes must blossom in his heart. He must build heaven within
his own inner heart. The good qualities within his inner
heart are what will serve him on the Day of Reckoning
(*Qiyāmah*). A person's good qualities and good thoughts will
become the celestial beings who will later perform service
(*qismat*) to him in the hereafter (*ākhirah*), and their appearance
will be that of innocent children. Even while in this world,
his qualities must perform service (*qismat*) to him. If he serves
the people in this world with his good qualities, those same
good qualities will serve him in the hereafter.

Therefore, it is his good qualities which become the
powers (*wilāyāt*), and that will serve him in the hereafter. But
if that river does not flow in one's heart here in this life, then
there is no river that flows in heaven. Man's worship (*'ibādat*)
becomes the garlanded swing. Only the fullness and plenitude of true prayer will give him these benefits. If he does
not achieve that here, he will not find it there.

This is why the river of milk which is compassion
should flow through man while he is here. Every sweet taste
of divine knowledge (*'ilm*) should flow through him, and the
river of Allah's grace should gush and flow within his heart
while he is here. He must build the house called heaven
while he is here. He should build that house with Allah's
qualities. Allah's qualities are that house and if those qualities
are not within him here, then he will not find them there.
There is a river of nectar, the river of Allah's divine knowledge (*'ilm*). It is a river in which one becomes intoxicated in
Allah, intoxicated by His *'ilm*, by His words, and by His
truth. There are three rivers: a river of milk, a river of honey,
and a river of divine nectar. Man's own qualities become the

precious gems, and His actions become the beauty of his house in the hereafter. There are many things like this which have been described. If these rivers do not flow in man's heart here in this lifetime, he will not find them there in the hereafter. These are things I have seen.

Questioner: Allah, *Subhānahu wa ta'ālā,* said in the Qur'an, "After death I will purify some people and take them to heaven." An Arab man said yesterday that when referring to the period between death and the day of reckoning (*qiyāmah*), Allah said, "Whoever says *'Lā ilāha ill-Allāhu'* will enter heaven," but He did not say when.

Bawa Muhaiyaddeen: When a man has complete trust (*tawakkul*) in Allah, he dies before death. When such a man physically dies and is buried in his grave, he attains the plenitude of eternal life (*hayāt*). That is his day of reckoning (*qiyāmah*). He dies, is placed in the grave (*qabr*), and is immediately given an eternal life. That is his day of reckoning. For each man this day of death and his day of reckoning are in his own hands, under his own control. There is a later Day of Judgment, but his death (*maut*) and his reckoning (*qiyāmah*) are close to one another.

Maut, or death, occurs in the world, and then after burial the reckoning, or *qiyāmah,* occurs in the grave. A man in whom the world has died is a true believer (*mu'min*), and when such a man is buried, he is given eternal life and taken to heaven. But, if one dies while the world is still within him, then when he is placed in the grave, he is subject to questioning. If through this questioning it is found that he has done wrong, that he has not acquired the wealth of Allah (*daulat*), then he will remain in that grave until the final Judgment Day. His grave becomes a holding prison where he is kept until the final inquiry on Judgment Day.

If one has made the world die within him while in this

world itself, then as soon as he is placed in the grave and the mourners walk seven steps away, he is brought back to life immediately, and that moment becomes his day of reckoning (*qiyāmah*). The inquiry is immediate. When they wake him in the grave, his light and beauty and the treasure he acquired from Allah will be revealed. He is given eternal life (*hayāt*) and is taken immediately from the grave. This is how it might be.

There is another Judgment Day, a final Judgment Day. If a person dies while the world is still within him, then the questioning is in the grave itself, and he is kept there until the final Judgment Day. Everything he says will be written down. Then he will have to remain in that holding prison.

I have spoken to many people like this in the grave, people from all four religions. They have told me how it happens. I explained this in the first mystical experience.[1] I have seen them face to face and spoken with them. In that mystical experience I explain how I fought with satan, and then I provide certain explanations. I stood near a tree and talked with those who came by. As I spoke to them from the foot of the graves, each one would say, "You have received the wealth of Allah (*daulat*). You have left the world behind and you are now close to Allah. Therefore, you lack nothing. Allah's grace (*rahmat*) functions for you." Then they would tell me their story. I continued past the graves of people from all the different religions and finally came to the cemetery of Islam, or *Furqān*. There they said the same thing.

People from all religions gathered around me and asked, "Please beg Allah to set us on the right path, O good one!"

I told them, "I will ask Allah. I will beg Him to help you."

They complained to me, "It is because of Allah that we

---

1. See footnote 1 on page 105.

have peace, but there is a *shaitān,* a demon, who grabs three or four of us daily. Our numbers are getting smaller because this satan eats us up. Soon there will be no one left."

I asked, "Where does he come from?"

And they replied, "From a twin well. It is from that region that he comes."

"I will see that he does not come again," I replied. Then I went toward the well. I picked a tall bamboo stalk and sharpened it. The well has two openings. When the *shaitān* poked his head out, I stabbed him with the stick and sent him right down to the lowest world. That lowest world is the place of the sexual arts (*līlas*) and illusion, the place from which we are born. It is the place of the arts and sensual pleasures—this was the twin well. There is a well outside and a well inside. The place from which we are born is the twin well. We take form in the inner well and come out. I killed that *shaitān* right in the well itself. This has been described in the first mystical experience.

We say people have died and are in the grave; these people may have done a measure of good or a measure of bad. Depending on the wealth (*daulat*) they receive from God in this world, a proportionate amount of nourishment (*rizq*) will be sent down to them. Even in the grave, Allah gives them nourishment. Allah does not only give us food here while we are alive, He sends nourishment even to those in the grave. But only if they have attained a certain state do they receive this nourishment. According to the extent of their search, they will be given the appropriate nourishment (*rizq*). Allah's kingdom is vast, but He does not forget to supply food even to the toad that lives under a rock. The difficulty is to see Him, but His grace and powers (*rahmat* and *wilāyāt*) are doing duty continually. This we can certainly see and understand, although we may not be able to see Him directly.

Questioner: There is a *hadīth* that the *Rasūl* ☝ said, "Those who dwell in heaven will see Allah, *Subhānahu wa ta`ālā*, every morning as if they would see Him with their own physical eyes. He will be seen clearly by everyone."

Bawa Muhaiyaddeen: When the *Rasūl* ☝ went on *Mi`rāj*,[2] Allah spoke to him from behind a veil. They discussed everything, with this veil between them. They discussed prayer and worship, and Allah told the *Rasūl* ☝ to tell his followers what they had discussed. The veil was still between them.

Then the *Rasūl* ☝ said, "Allah, I want to see You. I must see You!"

When the entire conversation was over, Allah said, "Take away this veil and look." And the *Rasūl* ☝ saw a mirror, only a mirror. It was of such brilliance, he could see the eighteen thousand universes in it. It was light. When he looked in the mirror he saw himself; he saw only his form, his beauty. He looked like a sixteen-year-old youth with a pointed moustache and a very beautiful, radiant face. It was his own beauty he saw in that mirror.

Therefore, what Prophet Muhammad ☝ saw when he went on *Mi`rāj* was his own beauty. The rest of the time, Muhammad ☝ only heard the speech and words that came from God. When one is in that state how does one see Allah? Allah is a mirror. A man sees only himself. If he sees Allah's beauty in himself, if he sees all of Allah's qualities and actions in himself, then Allah is a mirror, a light. When he looks inside that, he will see only his own beauty, the beauty of a sixteen-year-old who is eternally youthful.

When he returned from the *Mi`rāj*, Muhammad's ☝

---

followers asked if he had seen Allah. His wife and daughter, Khadijah and Fātimah ☺, also asked. But they would not have understood, so the *Rasūl* ☺ replied, "No, I did not see Him." In fact, he did not see Allah. But to 'Umar Ibnul-Khattāb ☺ he revealed the real secret; Muhammad ☺ told 'Umar ☺ alone what he had seen. This is the only person to whom he revealed this.

Therefore, one who does not see Allah within himself will never see Allah outside. If he is one who has seen Allah within, then he will see Allah outside. And what will he see? He will see himself. His own inner heart (*qalb*) will be his mirror, and when he looks in that mirror, he will see himself. He will see himself within the light of that mirror.

This may be the way it is, but we have not reached that state where we can speak to God.

March 26, 1979

18

JUDGMENT IN THE GRAVE

------·-·◁∞▷·-··------

Bawa Muhaiyaddeen: There is a Day of Judgment when all of creation will be raised up after the whole world is destroyed. The animals and the human-animals who were sent to hell in punishment will be raised up in their specific forms. On the appointed day all the beings in hell and heaven are raised up. All the energies, earth, gold, everything will be raised up. There is an appointed day for that. We cannot talk about it now. We will talk about it another day.

Question: Is there one Judgment Day for everyone or is each one judged when they die?

Bawa Muhaiyaddeen: When the food and water kept on earth for each individual finishes, he dies and is buried. The day he is placed in his grave is his own day of judgment. He is raised up on that day. Once he is buried, the angels Munkar and Nakīr ☺ come down to his grave. Until the body is placed in the grave it is as if that person was given chloroform; the dead person can still hear everything.

At the time of death, the Angel of Death comes. He has a kind of chloroform. As soon as that anesthesia is given, the person's life is finished. The mouth is closed, the eyes are closed, the ears are closed, and the tongue is halted. They are all under the effect of the chloroform. All the nerves stop functioning. There is no outward sound. The person cannot speak. He does not take a breath and he cannot see anything. His outward functions have stopped, but everything

163

that is taking place around him is still being perceived within. He cannot speak, he does not breathe, and he cannot see, but everything is being perceived within. Sounds can be heard, but the body cannot speak. Everything that is happening around him, how the mourners are wailing, shouting, and talking, how they are scolding him, how much they are eating, everything can be perceived by the person who died. It is the same during an operation; the patient under the anesthesia may hear the cutting and the stitching sound. The person who has died also hears everything, but he does not speak, so people think he is just dead.

So for the time between a person's death in this world and his burial in the grave, he is under anesthesia. As soon as he is laid in the grave he is given another injection, an antidote, and the effect of the chloroform is taken away. Then he sits up and the two angels, Munkar and Nakīr ☺, ask him questions. "Who are you? What did you do? Whose son are you? What are the things that you have done?" They will ask the eyes, "What did you see? What did you do?" Every one of the organs will be questioned. They will ask each of the twenty-eight letters in the body. That is the Qur'an. That never dies and is eternal (hayāt).

So the two angels will ask every organ—eyes, nose, ears, teeth, tongue, hands, legs—and inquire into the faults committed by each one of them individually. Each part of the body will answer, and the two angels on either shoulder[1] will deliver what they have written. They will provide the evidence and say, "At this breath he said this. In this time he said this." And so on, they will give the evidence.

Then the person in the grave is asked to write what the eyes did. There is no paper to write on, so the white burial

---

1. Raqib and Atīd ☺ are the angels who record the good and evil a person does during his lifetime.

shroud is used as paper. So he writes.

The forefinger is the writing finger, the *kalimah* finger. It is impermissible (*harām*) to add lime to betel leaf[2] with this finger. If you do, it will shrivel up, its point will be wasted, and you will not have a pen to write with. That is why we take lime with the middle or ring finger.

So the forefinger is the pen. Then what do you do? There is no ink. You are told, "You have your own ink to write with. That is your saliva. Touch your pen to your own saliva and that is the ink for you to write with." As soon as everything is written, your *qiyāmah* (reckoning) is finished.

Qiyāmah is the time in this world. That is, you appeared and now this is the end of that birth. Your *qiyāmah* is the end of that cycle, and what is left for you is your grave. Your cycle on earth is finished, and you have to wait until the final Judgment Day in this grave. Until that day, you will be given punishment in the grave according to what you have done. The angels will come, snakes will come, scorpions will come, and you will receive lashes for each thing you did. Everything you did before, everything that you did to others, will come back to you in turn. If you had hit somebody before, you will be lashed now. If you did something with your eyes before, you will get that back. You have to accept all that punishment and wait. Until the Day of Judgment, you have to suffer this torture and torment.

Judgment Day is when God gives His judgment. Until then, you receive the judgment for whatever you have done. There will be snakes, scorpions, and various reptiles. The day when all lives are raised from the dead is the final Day of Judgment, and until that time this grave is your prison. While there, each person will be given all that he has earned.

---

2. In the East the leaf of the betel plant is chewed with a little lime and areca nut.

That is the time in the grave.
    Do you understand?

Question: If you are born and reborn again in different forms, when it comes to the final day, which of these forms is given judgment?

Bawa Muhaiyaddeen: There are seventy-three groups. Out of those seventy-three groups, only one consists of true human beings. The other seventy-two are in the form of animals. They are half-human, half-animal, in the form of beasts and monkeys and other creatures. All of these people have to be born and reborn. They die and go to the super-market, and then they must come back to the world. Like a bull, as soon as they finish plowing, they go to the supermar-ket and then back again. They are recycled back and forth, first plowing, then to the supermarket, and then to the table.

    This Judgment Day is meant only for the human being. Out of seventy-three groups, those which are half-man and half-beast have to be recycled and reborn again and again. They are beasts, they have their own king, and that king is god for them. If each animal worships his own king as his god, he has to be born again. He is not a human being. If someone worships a demon, it is that demon that is being born again. If you worship various forms of *asuras*, they have to drink your blood. If you worship dogs, that is an animal and it has to return to the supermarket and come back again. That god has to come back and the person who is worship-ing that god also has to come back. That is how it works.

    Whatever somebody keeps as a substitute for God, as opposite to Him, and worships, he has to merge with that. If fire is somebody's god, then he has to return to fire in hell. If water is their god, they have to come back to water. If it is air, they have to come back to air. If illusion (*māyā*) is their god, they have to come back to that. Those are the rebirths.

But God's judgment is for man. Judgment is only for the human being. That is a very subtle point.

It is so rare, rarest of the rare, to be born as a human being. It is so very rare. And out of these, to be born without blemish and deformity is still rarer. Even more rare is to be born as a male. Even more rare is to be born as one of knowledge. Even rarer is to be born a king. And still rarer than that is to be born as a *gnāni,* one who has gained divine wisdom. So when you say rare, it is extremely rare, something that is almost impossible to attain. A man who does not need judgment is so very rare to find. That is one group.

You are the ones who need to be judged. Isn't there a judgment for us? Are you the one in ten million who does not need to be judged? No, you are not. A judgment is necessary. You are a human being, and I am a human being. You come in this room, and for the short space of time that you are here, you may be a true man. But then after you leave you may act like a demon. Another time you may be a doctor. Another time you stray further and you turn into *māyā* (illusion), or you stray further out and you turn into a demon who takes lives. Another time you give in to the base desires (*nafs*) and turn into a dog of desire, or you stray still further and turn into a bloodsucking vampire or a lion. So a judgment is required, isn't it? Only at one short point in time were you a true man. All the other times you were changing into various forms. So a judgment is necessary. If you have turned totally into a true man, then you are God. So why would darkness come to the sun?

Question: If we suffer so much in the grave, what more judgment do we need?

Bawa Muhaiyaddeen: It is not like that. That is a different point. You were a beast at one time, and you were meting out judgment or punishment on other animals and other lives. For that you will be kept in that animal form, and you will suffer the same torment you caused others when you were in that form. This goes on for seven years. Another time you were a snake and you caused suffering, and so for a further seven years, you will be given the punishment for what you did as a snake. Then you will not be in a human form, you will be in a snake form. Another time you were in a tiger form, drinking blood and eating flesh. That form will appear and you will have to suffer in that form for seven years. Another time you lived as an elephant, and you will suffer for seven years in that form for what you did. This is what is given according to what was written.

For each of the forms that you took in your life, you will have to undergo suffering for seven years. It will take that long to go through all that. If you had remained a true man the whole time, then nothing would happen in the grave. If you did not take all these forms and had remained a true man, then you would be light, you would be God, you would be a representative of God. So there would be no suffering in that grave. You would be a king in all the inner realms in the world. As a king you would perform your duties, protecting and helping others wherever it was needed. Your grave would be a great big mansion, a palace for you, and there would be so many people performing service to you. The heavenly beings would be there, and so much would be done for you. That would be a palace of the Trustee. You would be dwelling there and traveling all around the inner realms, as a true man offering help and protection.

Whatever, this is my craziness. I have not been there to see it yet.

Question: Occasionally, soon after some people have died, Bawa has said that they are in a good place. Does it mean that for some it is possible to escape all this?

Bawa Muhaiyaddeen: I might have said that, but what else can I say? Because someone asked, I might have said that a person was in a good place.

Suppose somebody begs and asks, "*Aiyō*, where is my father, is he in a good place?" These are divine secrets, so what can one say? You don't know about the heavenly kingdom or about the suffering. So if I tell you the truth about that you will pelt me with stones because of your attachment. You will throw stones at me and bite my nose off. So what must I say to save myself? I will say, "Oh, they are in a good place according to what they have done, each of them." That is what I have to say, "They are in a good place. They are in whatever place they have built for themselves. You should not worry about this." There are many meanings I cannot tell. I know where they are, but it isn't possible to tell you exactly. To make you happy, to comfort you, I tell you that they are in a good place according to what they have done.

If I applied perfume on your shirt and your nose, they will certainly have that scent, but does that fragrance travel lower down? It is applied only for one section. Did I apply perfume all over your body? No, so all the rest of your body will not have the scent. The foul odor will still be there down below. That foul odor still has to be worked on; the full body has not been cleared yet. But the person has handed back his debt to the earth; the body was not given to the fire. That alone is a great debt which he has repaid in full. He was not given to the fire. Out of the five shareholders, he has given back the share to the earth. That is an achievement.

November 30, 1977

19

REACHING THE REALM BEYOND ATTACHMENTS

Question: Is there a place in heaven where we will recognize our relatives?

Bawa Muhaiyaddeen: If you have those attachments at the time you leave this world, then you will not go to *barzakhul-'ālam*.[1] You will not find any room there. Only if all the things of this world die away from you will you reach *barzakhul-'ālam*. Otherwise you will reach the realm of the elements of earth, fire, water, air, and ether, and your judgment will be rendered to you there.

Question: Do we have a judgment day on the day we die or is there another Judgment Day for all souls?

Bawa Muhaiyaddeen: As soon as the state of death overtakes a person, he is given his judgment in his grave. Each one's *qiyāmah*, his reckoning, is finished in his grave. The angels Munkar and Nakīr ☺ raise him up and question him. That is his *qiyāmah*.

The Day of *Qiyāmah*, is sometimes used to refer to the final Judgment Day. On that day all of everything will be raised up, and that is when you must hand over the scroll, or account, that was written on your behalf at the time you

---

1. The sphere or realm between this world and the hereafter. The place where the soul is contained in the body between the time of death and the time it is raised from the grave is known as *barzakhul-'ālam*. See glossary.

171

were questioned in the grave. Then you will be raised up in
the form of the qualities you acted with in the world. If you
had the qualities of a bull, you will be raised up in the form
of a bull. If you had the qualities of a dog, you will be raised
up in the form of a dog. If you had the qualities of a monkey,
you will be raised up in the form of a monkey. If you had the
qualities of a snake, you will be raised up in the form of a
snake, and so on. In this way, your form will change, and
you will be raised up in the form of the qualities you had
when you were in the world. If you spent your life drinking
and imbibing intoxicants, your tongue will be lolling out like
a dog's. If you ate things that were impermissible (harām), you
will be raised up in the form of a pig. This is what happens
on the Day of Qiyāmah, the final Day of Judgment.

On this day, Allah keeps the Rasūl, Prophet Muhammad ﷺ,
on his left side and tells him to survey the scene. Allah points
toward hell and says, "Are any of your followers there?
Look." Then the Prophet ﷺ will beg God to forgive his
followers.

Each individual's qiyāmah is completed in his own grave.
Those who have attachments remain here in this world; they
do not go to barzakhul-'ālam.

Mankind is divided into seventy-three groups. Out of
these only one group goes directly to barzakhul-'ālam without
having to face any questions. These are people who have no
attachment. They have died while still in the world, while
still alive.

January 19, 1981

PART THREE

The Sufi Way of Life

OPEN YOUR HEART BEFORE
YOU REACH YOUR DEATH

————————⟨∞⟩————————

*Yā Allāh, the Almighty One, who created the
skies and the earth,
The One who created the moon that grows from
crescent to full,
Having created a covering called day and night,
You placed the world within it.
Within the world You placed everything,
And then to realize all things,
You placed the wisdom within man (insān).*

*You, O Allah, are the wisdom within the wisdom
of man,
The One who created the universe ('ālam)
and all of everything.
You are the One who resplends as everything.
You, O Allah, who are my Lord, are life itself, my
very life.
You are the Treasure that knows my thoughts and
my intentions.
You are my Chieftain who knows everything
about me.
To all of creation You are the Primal One,
You are the Creator, You are the Emperor who rules*

everything created.
You are the Leader who realizes the truth,
And You are the Dearest One who is the life
     within all lives.

You are the One who knows what truth is,
And You are the One who has understood who the
     Lone One is.
You are the One who knows what truth is,
And You are the One who has understood that You are
     the Lone One.
You are the One who has created a parallel for
     everything in the world.
You are the Lord for the world of the souls (arwāh)
     and the hereafter (ākhirah).
For both stations, the here and the hereafter,
You are the Light, the Resplendent One who asks
     the questions.
You are the life of my soul,
You are the light of my wisdom,
You are the clarity of my wisdom.

Having placed the secret (sirr) called the world
And having placed the covering of night and darkness,
This world (dunyā) and the hereafter (ākhirah),
You placed within all things the blissful honey and
     the tastes.

You placed within the two parts called good and bad,

That which is tasteful and that which is repulsive.

To reduce or expand the world, You placed the

   intellect and the various levels of wisdom.

Within, You placed desire and torpor, justice and

   injustice, clarity and ignorance.

Then to help us know with clarity, You placed

The one Prophet and the certitude of absolute

   faith (īmān).

You gave us these to enable us to recite the kalimah[1]

And to accept the truth of the Prophet,

To enable us to accept that he is the Causal Prophet,[2]

   the Messenger,

And to believe that Allah is the Complete One.

You gave us these

To enable us to worship God,

Saying that there is none else,

To protect all lives as our own,

To give charity to every life,

To understand fasting for Allah alone,

And to realize all lives as our own,

And feed them with that nectar.

---

1. The affirmation of faith—*Lā ilāha ill-Allāhu:* There is nothing other than You, O God. Only You are Allah.
2. *Kārana Nabī*

Then for those who still do not understand the truth,
You also gave the duty of pilgrimage (hajj),
So that they will accept Islam, at least at the end,
Before death comes to overtake them
And before the gathering on Judgment Day
    (mahshar),
And so that they may realize the faults within themselves.

O man, you are within the two coverings of this
    world.
You grew up within the covering of death, this world,
    and the hereafter.
The death and the desire that are within you have
    covered you.
If you realize this within, you will perceive many
    tastes, sorrows, and joys.
O man, realize the secrets contained within.
There are the gems of wisdom, who are the prophets,
The favorites of God (auliyā'),
The ones who explain with wisdom (qutbs),
And the one hundred and twenty-four thousand
    messengers.
Within you there are also millions of creations with
    different forms.
There are satans, ghosts, demons, animals, and
    beasts, snakes and scorpions, centipedes,
And so many different kinds of insects that come

to bite you.

These are really your thoughts that come to tear and
nip at you.
The fire and the wind that eat away at you,
The fire, the wind, and all the lives that come to
attach you in so many millions of forms
Are your own thoughts!
They will eat you, burn you, torture you, and subject
you to suffering.
The four hundred trillion, ten thousand spiritual
thoughts come as animals,
As demons and ghosts, as witches and ogres.
All of them come to attack you as countless millions
of demons and ghosts.
They will tear at you and devour you.
All the ghosts and the demons that you raised
Will eat you, bite you, tear at you, and gobble you up.

When every one of your qualities is destroying you,
You will realize within yourself what joy is and what
sorrow is.
Then you will realize that it is your very thoughts
that will devour you,
Your very desires that will kill you,
Your attachments that will cause you to suffer.
Your fanaticism is what will burn you up.
Ignorance is what will torment you,

And your obstinacy will topple you into the fire.
Your lust will burn your very self,
Your anger, lust, and greed will burn and roast you.
Your anger is what will drag you into hell,
And all of your thoughts will make you suffer.
All these things made you forget Allah
And only gave you pleasure in nourishing your body.
These things made you grow,
But they made you forget the One who created you
   and nourished you,
Protected you and gave you life.
You forgot the One who is the Leader for all lives,
The One who will ask you questions on the Day of
   Reckoning (Qiyāmah).
You forgot Allah, the One with the benevolent gaze.
You forgot to pray to Allah.

This is how you have behaved.
You preferred satan and demons and ghosts.
You wanted to own everything in the world,
And making these things your possessions,
You considered them your happiness
And enjoyed their taste.
Just as the snake keeps the poison within its
   own mouth,
You kept hell and sin and satan's qualities within
   your heart and mind.

You kept them in your life, in your qualities, in your
  actions, and in your mouth.

You who have relished and enjoyed their taste,
Do you not realize that these are the very things that
  will torment you?
Do you not realize this?
Do you not realize how these can ensnare you,
  O man?
You, who came here to understand everything,
Are now hesitant to understand even yourself.
You succumbed to the evil things
And planted the flag of injustice.
O man, you have become a wretched one
Who schemes to act with injustice in the world.
Your tongue will destroy you,
Your mind and the scenes of your mind will ruin you
And make you subject to so many torments
  and agonies.

So open the covering of your life and look within,
Open your heart and look within,
See what is tasty, what is bliss,
What will kill you and what will be victorious.
See and realize what is good and what is bad,
Worship your Lord,
Think of Him,

And look meltingly at Him, O man.
Give up the form of the beast,
Take on the form of a human being (insān),
Set out courageously to live as a true
    believer (mu'min).
Have certitude and hold fast to the kalimah and to
    absolute faith.
Follow a learned wise man,
Join him and learn wisdom.
Take the key that opens your heart
    and see the clarity.

Open the covering of this world and the hereafter,
See the secret room of the essence (dhāt) and the
    manifestation (sifāt),
Open that box and see Allah's qualities,
See the attachments of the world
And the compassionate qualities of Allah that are
    without attachment.
See selfishness and pride
And then see the unselfish qualities of Allah.
Realize all this, O man.

O man, if you realize this state,
You will know what true joy is
And what is truly tasty.
From that you can derive sweetness and happiness.

You will see the state of considering all lives
    as your own life,
And you will realize that God is but One.
When you realize this with wisdom,
You will understand the universe ('ālam), the world
    of the souls (arwāh), and all of everything.
You will see the connection between Allāhu and
    man (insān),
And you will understand the state of prayer which is
    a direct communication between man and Allah.
You will attain the connection that is your birthright.
You will perceive the resonance of the constant
    remembrance of God (dhikr)
And the greetings of peace (salāms) and the
    supplications (salawāt)
To that Effulgent One who is Allah.
You will hear the resonance of the salāms
    and the salawāt
Of the heavenly beings, the prophets, and Allah.

Hearing this, the human being (insān) who
    gives salāms
Will hear the voice of the One who is the Lord
    of everything,
And his heart (qalb) will flourish with the joy of
    knowing the sound of Allah.
Then he will see his heart open,

And he will hear the worship to that One who is Allah.

Open your heart before you reach your death,
Open that room
And seek to take the pearl of truth out of the
 darkness.
Drive away your attachments,
Drive away that hell,
And seek the help of Allah
To lift you out of that hell.
For the path of bliss to open before you
And to make your wisdom resplend,
Seek the help of Allah, always.
Āmīn. Yā Rabbal-'ālamīn.
May You protect us, O Lord of the universes.
As-salāmu 'alaikum. Āmīn.
May the peace of God be with you. So be it.

April 15, 1985

20

THE WONDER THAT IS MAN

Man is an extraordinary being. He is the one who has been endowed with and can realize the wealth of the hereafter (*ākhirah*). The human being is, therefore, a miraculous wonder that is deserving of praise in the hereafter. If man can receive that wealth and manifest it even while he is here in this world, then his life will be filled with that praise, and he will be praised by Allah in this present life itself. This state is the unchanging wealth in man's life, and one who has attained this will have earned Allah's grace (*rahmat*).

This wealth belongs to man and man must realize this. If, however, one born as a human being lives without receiving this wealth or realizing this state, that is an even greater wonder. Why? There is life and death (*hayāt* and *maut*). One who receives Allah's wealth has eternal life, while one who lives as a wondrous being who does not receive this wealth has actually died. He has changed from the state of a human being. Man should realize this with his wisdom. He must realize what the state of true man (*insān*) should be. He should realize what death is and what eternal life is. This has been explained in the revelations and the warnings given to us by the prophets, and in the wisdom and the determined faith (*īmān*) imparted to us by them.

Death and eternal life are within man's hands at all times. He should understand both and realize that death exists within him at every moment. Every one of the four hundred trillion, ten thousand qualities within him are

185

qualities that can cause his death. Through these qualities
whatever he searches for in the world, whatever he intends,
whatever he gathers, and whatever he hoards only lead to his
death. Every breath is a breath of death. Everything he eats,
looks at, acts upon, sits on, or thinks about can bring death
to him before the blinking of an eye. His desires, his actions,
his cravings, his anger, hastiness, impatience, the arrogance
of the 'I', the base desires (*nafs ammārah*), and the qualities of
lust, hatred, and miserliness, all point him toward death
every second. Attachments, blood ties, and the divisions of 'I'
and 'you'; the differences of race, religion, and color; the love
of possessions, property, and livestock; the separations of my
belongings and your belongings, my kingdom and your
kingdom, my food and your food—each one of these
thoughts warn him of his impending death.

A slight change in his breath while sleeping can cause a
man to die. If he shouts with great excitement, "Ha! This is
mine!" that very joy can cause his death. Or if he fails to
attain something he yearns for, that sorrow can kill him. If
he takes too much or too little of something, he can become
ill and die. He can choke on the very water he drinks. If he
laughs too hard or if he swallows too much food at once, he
can choke and die.

Everything man desires and gathers in this world,
everything he thinks about and intends, whatever he eats,
even what he looks at can be the cause of his death within
the blinking of an eye. All the things he desires change
continually, but death never changes or leaves him. It can
come to him any second, without the slightest warning,
whatever he may be doing, whether he is flying in the skies
or walking on the earth, when he is sitting or when he is
sleeping. But man, not realizing that he is holding death in
his hands, holds on to the world, and as a result he suffers
every moment of his life. With every breath, in both happi-

ness and sorrow, he suffers and cries.

Human beings (insān) must realize this. The animals, reptiles, and birds do not do this; they do not have this quality. They place their trust in God and seek only what is required at any given time (waqt). They conduct their lives without any worry of tomorrow and with the belief that Allah is sufficient. But man has forgotten this state. He has forgotten his impending death, and he has forgotten Allah. Man lets go of Allah's words and His kingdom and treats the world as the ultimate treasure. This is the wonder! There is no other wonder. At all times, man holds on to his inevitable death as his possession and forfeits his true possession which is eternal life. He lets go of life and accepts death. Even though man comes into the world and receives many treasures, he considers death to be his most valuable possession. This is a great wonder. There is no wonder greater than this.

There are four things a human being (insān) must ponder:

First: "I am one who is subject to death. When I die, will I die as one of true faith (mu'min) or as one who does not believe (kāfir)? Will I die in a state of darkness or will I die in a state of light?" Before we die we must understand this with our wisdom.

Second: "I was formed as a fetus in the earth. I was born in the earth, I ate the things of the earth, and I have grown up with the elements—earth, fire, water, air, ether, or illusion (māyā). Finally, I will be laid back into the same earth from which I came and become prey to that earth again. On the day of reckoning (qiyāmah) I will be raised up, and when they question me in the grave, will what they write on my behalf be good or bad? Will it be a day of eternal life and light (hayāt) or a day of death and darkness (maut)? What will they write on my behalf?" While we are still in this grave called the world, before being laid in the grave of the earth, we must find out the answer to these questions.

Third: "The final Day of Reckoning (*Qiyāmah*) and its results connect me with Allah. On that day called *Qiyāmah*, my time in the grave is over. I will have to rise up with the scroll and speak with Allah. At that time, will the scroll I take with me contain good or bad? And in which hand will I carry this final decree? Will the scroll, containing the good and the bad written on my behalf, be placed in my left hand or my right hand?"

Before we die we must understand this Day of Reckoning and know in which hand we will receive the results of this questioning. Worship and service (*'ibādat*), the remembrance of God (*dhikr*), contemplation of God (*fikr*), prayer, and intending and focusing on God, all these must rise from within us, speak with Allah, and know what He is going to award us.

Fourth: "Finally when the judgment comes, will God give me heaven or hell? What will happen when I place this scroll in Allah's hands, when I meet and speak with Allah face to face for my judgment?"

With wisdom we must understand right from wrong, rise from this grave which is the world, and understand what is going to be written on our behalf. We must understand and write down our final judgment by meeting Allah directly in our worship and service (*'ibādat*) and in our prayers (*vanakkam*). We must find out the details of our judgment by dying before our death, and if we can discover the answers to these questions while we are still in this world, then we will attain eternal life. That is the judgment. However, if we fail to obtain these answers while we are here, then we will have to die and go to the grave in the earth.

If one understands whether he will die as a true believer or as a non-believer, then he is one who is known as a realized human being (insān kāmil), a representative of Allah, a slave of Allah, one who has surrendered to Allah. But if man fails to realize this, he dies within one breath and is reborn in the next breath. He dies in one intention and is reborn in the next intention. He dies with one look and is reborn with the next look. Out of his thoughts and desires, he creates four hundred trillion, ten thousand forms within himself and then worships these as gods. If he has snake-like thoughts, he creates an idol of a snake and worships it. He worships his own thoughts and these idols are his "thought-gods." If he has arrogance, then he creates the form of an elephant and worships that elephant. If he has the deceitful qualities of a rat, he creates a rat form and worships it. He makes every one of these forms and then worships their qualities which are opposite to Allah's. Like this, he experiences one hundred and five million deaths and births each day. This is what is called karma. This is why the world is called his grave.

Man dies in the grave of this world and is reborn every second because of his thoughts. Only when he gives up these thoughts and lives his life with complete trust in Allah (tawakkul 'alallāh) will he escape from that grave and receive the eternal life of the hereafter and the wealth and grace of all the universes (rahmatul-'ālamīn). Failure to realize this is the wonder of man! Every second of his life he holds death in his hand, and still he tries to carry the entire world with him. Before the blinking of an eye, before one breath leaves and the next one comes, he tries to grab something else. The wonder is that man, born so exalted, born as a human being (insān), has come to such a state. Instead of seeking wisdom, he tries to hold on to the changing things in the world. This is karma. This is the karma that came with him in his body. Only a man who can cut away this karma can overcome his death and attain the state of eternal life. Every one of us must reflect on this. To die before death—that is the most exalted state.

Apart from Allah and truth, everything else man desires and nurtures within himself will eventually kill him. Whatever he is in love with now will cause him sorrow and then kill him. Whatever he places his trust in is the very thing that will kill him tomorrow and take its share. Whatever he fosters in the world, that same thing will kill him. Whatever he desires will kill him and take a share. These are the things that cause him grief, illness, and suffering. They will lead only to his death and his rebirth. But if man holds on solely to Allah, His qualities, actions, and state, His duties and the wealth of His grace, that will be his freedom, his beauty, and his resplendent light. That will be his wealth. That will give him a life free of want and the plenitude of eternal life. A man in such a state will not cause pain to another, and therefore, there is nothing that will want to consume him and take its share of him. Such a one is a true man, a perfected being (insān kāmil). But all the time he does not realize this he is worse than a beast. The animals have at least attained a certain state, they place their trust in God and take their food.

This is why Prophet Muhammad, the Rasūlullāh ﷺ, said, "Go even unto China to learn divine knowledge ('ilm)." Learn wisdom. If one has that wisdom, he becomes a true human being (insān), but if he gives up that wisdom, he is worse than a beast. That is his death. Every thought is his death. This is what every one of my children must think about. We must understand eternal life and death. Āmīn.

May Allah give us this wisdom and the wealth of His qualities and explanations, so that we can attain the state of death before death. May He give us the wealth and grace of eternal life. May He give us His qualities, His grace, His treasures, and the wealth of the three worlds. May He bestow upon us that resplendent light of wisdom and absolute faith, certitude, and determination *(īmān)*, and may He lift us up with His gracious hands. May it be so, O Ruler of the universes. *(Āmīn, Yā Rabbal-'ālamīn.)*

December 6, 1979

21

SCALES OF JUDGMENT

———————··◦∞◦··———————

My sheikh once told me, "Don't ever think that you have finished your development. All the ascetics (*munivars*), all those capable of performing magic (*sitthars*), those who fly in the sky and those who live on the earth, those who have studied many things, the celestial beings (*dēvas*), and the wise men (*gnānis*) were finally brought down and subjugated by the place of birth. Having done everything in the house of hell, they finally reach hell and succumb to it. What they finally attain is hell.

"In truth, you can receive God's grace within a second. Within a second everything you have searched for and attained can be destroyed. You can be destroyed in an instant. You can change in an instant. The seven hells (*jahannam*) can be yours or you can reach God in a moment. When you disappear in that state, you can be with God in an instant. In life, within a second you can lose your divine knowledge (*'ilm*), and within a second you can lose your faith, determination, and certitude. You can lose all these things and be destroyed in a second by the differences of 'I' and 'you', the differences of one's own property and relatives, the differences of race and religion, the differences due to pride, the differences caused by envy, jealousy, and selfishness, and the differences of hunger, old age, disease, blood ties, and illusion (*māyā*).

"In a second you can reach the seven hells or in a second you can reach God. Between birth and death, each

193

second awaits you. It takes but an instant to destroy everything you have searched for and acquired, and it takes but an
instant to realize everything you have searched for. Until
you die, each second of your life is in this state. Be careful.
Hold on. Do not let go of your grasp or deviate from your
path at any moment." This is the essence of what my sheikh
told me.

My sheikh is not of this world. He is one of true wealth
(daulat), a sheikh connected to the hereafter (ākhirah). Therefore, nothing he said will ever fail to occur. All the meanings
given by him exist as the truth from the time of creation
(awwal) to the time of the hereafter (ākhirah).

According to his explanations, if we deviate for even
one second on the path, if even one toe turns away from
where it should be placed, we will fall down. We need
dedication, concentration, balance, and wisdom (thānam,
nithānam, avathānam, and gnānam).

Dedicating or offering oneself to God in this world is
thānam. To walk on that path we need concentration or
nithānam. The connection between us and God is very, very
subtle. It is even subtler than one segment of a strand of hair
that has been split into seven. Such is the sharpness of
wisdom, a path with an extremely sharp edge. This is the
only path that connects us with God. Below this path are the
seven hells, the seven canals. These include the canals of
birth, karma, sin, illusion (māyā), and the sexual arts. The
canal of birth is the hell of fire, the vilest hell in which fire
rages constantly. Within it burns the fire of hunger, anger,
sin, karma, and birth, the fire of pride, arrogance, fanaticism,
race, and color, the fire of differences, jealousy, envy, and
selfishness, and the fire that arises from one's own possessions.

These are the fires of the vilest of canals. You entered
that canal and emerged from it. That is how you were born.

This is the fire of the canal of birth. You have to escape from this vilest of all canals. Snakes, scorpions, centipedes, cats, dogs, satan, ghosts, demons, base desires (*nafs*), selfish desires (*ammārah*), jinns, and fairies emerge from this canal. These are the animals that devour you. These are the snakes and scorpions that consume you. Escape from these poisons.

God has built a bridge over all these. This path leads to Him and is sharper than the edge of a sword and finer than a strand of hair that has been split seven times. Walk on this path. This is the bridge known as the Straight Path (*Sırātul-Mustaqīm*). You must walk on this bridge. This is where judgment will occur. The Messenger of God, the *Rasūlullāh* ☺, is here and this is where both your good and bad are weighed. Look at these scales. It is the balance known as *mizān trās*.

When you die, two wooden posts are placed at either end of your grave. They are called the *mizān* boards. The scale, or *mizān trās*, hangs between the post placed by your head and the post that is placed by your feet. This is the scale that will weigh your life. Perfectly pure faith (*īmān*) will tilt the scale toward the post at the head.

While you are still alive, even before you die, you have this scale of judgment, *mizān trās*. If you die as one of pure faith (*mu'min*), as one who knows the five and six duties of *dīnul-Islām* and *Īmān-Islām*,[1] then you will realize Allah's justice, the path of His justice, and the qualities of that path. This is the state I am trying to help you attain. Good and evil (*khair* and *sharr*), permissible and impermissible (*halāl* and *harām*), right and wrong, all of this will be seen within you. You have to discriminate and examine their weight. This is the *mizān*

---

1. *Dīnul-Islām*—the faith of surrender to the will of Allah. *Īmān-Islām*—the complete unshakeable faith of the pure heart directed toward the One God, trusting only in Him and worshiping only Him.

trās, the balance of discrimination, within you. Let this be the scale that weighs your inner heart (*qalb*).

Purity and truth balance and weigh things on this scale of the *mizān trās*. The light of Muhammad ⊕, the chosen Messenger (*Mustafar-Rasūl*), exists at the base of this *mizān trās*, in the ocean of divine knowledge (*bahrul-'ilm*). You can see him at the place where the balancing or weighing occurs.

The outcome depends on what your inner heart has established. If your heart has discarded what is bad, accepted and acted according to what is good, and has experienced the benefits and advantages of doing so; if your heart has acquired and acted according to divine knowledge ('*ilm*), to the ocean of divine knowledge, to Allah's grace (*rahmat*), peace, tranquility, His qualities, and His ninety-nine attributes; if you have done all this and have given peace and tranquility to others—then you will dispense justice with God's qualities. It is at this station of justice that you will see the *Rasūl* ⊕. This is where Muhammad ⊕ exists, at the foot of the *mizān trās*.

At the time when the *Rasūl* ⊕ had to leave the world and be transformed, he replied to a question asked by his followers, "You can see me at the foot of the *mizān trās*. That is where I will be." This scale exists as your inner heart (*qalb*). There is no other scale, only the *mizān trās*. The *Rasūl* ⊕ said, "You can see me at the foot of the scale, which weighs good and bad." When you discard evil and keep only the scale of goodness, you can see Allah and the *Rasūl* ⊕ at that place, and you will be able to cross the bridge. Only through the assistance of the *Rasūl* ⊕ can you cross that bridge. Only that grace can walk over that bridge. Otherwise you will not be able to cross. That is what was said.

The *Rasūl* ⊕ said, "I have brought the words of Allah, and I am giving those words as a gift (*hadīyah*) to you. I will give you Allah's treasure and depart. I will give you what He has given and leave. You should understand the meaning within these words. I will be at the foot of the *mizān trās*. You can meet me there."

We should understand good and bad and realize this *mizān trās* before we die. After we are buried this *mizān* board is firmly planted on our grave. This is also the board which is firmly planted within, once good and bad are understood. This *mizān trās* is absolute faith (*īmān*). Allah's grace will be impressed within that faith, and when His grace is written in this manner, the individuals are then known as people of pure faith (*mu'mins*). Prior to their physical death, they resplend as those with pure faith and die within Allah. This *mizān* board is a sign that a person has reached this state. The piece of wood that is planted on the grave is just an outward sign, but it is really planted while you are alive.

If you do not understand this while you are here, then all your actions will be actions of the seven hells (*jahannam*), and you will not see the *Rasūl* ⌣. If you see the *Rasūl* ⌣ at this place, hell will be moved far away from you. You will be able to transcend hell. If you do not see the *Rasūl* ⌣ at this place, hell will become yours. It is at the foot of the *mizān trās* that hell can either be pushed far away from you or be given to you. If you do not attain understanding at this place, then you will not go beyond hell. You will only attain hell.

Allah's *Rasūl* ⌣ said, "Those who have seen me will not see hell." We must understand this place of justice. We must think about this. If you try to walk on that bridge without reflecting on this and without that justice, that *mizān trās* in your hand, you will only end up swimming in hell, sin, base desires, religion, color, pride, possessiveness, anger, and other evils. This will only result in situations that will devour you tomorrow. We must understand this. These are the words of the wealth of Allah, the *Rasūl* ⌣, and the *Qutb* ⌣. Such is the wealth they have accumulated, and such are their words and actions.

As long as you do not understand this, as long as you do not realize the *mizān trās*, as long as you do not go beyond this, then every action of yours, every prayer that you perform without realizing the place of justice and without seeing the *Rasūl* ﷺ at the foot of the *mizān trās* will have you swimming in hell. This is all you will know. This means that you will not cross the bridge. Only if you see the *Rasūl* ﷺ at the foot of the *mizān trās* will you cross the bridge. You *can* see the *Rasūl* ﷺ at this place. But if at this place, you do not realize your own judgment, faith (*īmān*), and perfect purity, if you do not realize the qualities and wealth of a true believer, then you will not get that treasure.

In your search you must understand the right and wrong of each and every thing. Then you must walk across the bridge that is sharper than a sword, finer than God's qualities, finer than His grace and actions, wiser than wisdom, and more subtle than subtle. This bridge is subtler than divine knowledge (*'ilm*), subtler than the wisdom of divine knowledge (*'ilm*).

You must walk on that path and offer yourself to Allah (*thānam*). You should annihilate all things other than God (*fanā'*) and immerse yourself in Him (*baqā'*) and walk on His narrow path. You can be in this world, but the world should not be within you. You can perform the duties of the world, but the actions of the world should not be within you. You can do anything, but it should not be done by *you*. You can feed others, but you should not think that *you* have fed them. You can do good, but you should not think *you* have done it. Whatever you do should not be considered as having been done by *you*. You should immerse yourself in God (*baqā'*), and He should do the work.

Everything you see must be seen by Him. Everything you do should be done by Him. Everything you speak should be His speech. Everything you eat should be His food; it should be permissible (halāl). Your conduct should be His conduct. Everything you buy or give should be bought and given by Him. When He receives something, it is permissible (halāl); when you receive it, it is impermissible (harām). What He receives is good, what you receive is evil. What He does is good, what you do is bad. When He looks upon something it is a resplendent gaze; when you look at something, your gaze is envious and filled with illusion. All His embraces are embraces of justice and equality; your embraces are embraces of blood ties and karma. You must think about this.

If you try to do His work, karma will follow and take you to hell. You should first annihilate everything but Allah and then immerse yourself completely in Him. Surrender yourself to Him and then surrender within that surrender. This is baqā'. If you do not understand this state, if you do not see the needle of this scale, if you do not understand your own judgment, then you will be on the wrong side of the bridge and in a place from which you cannot transcend hell.

However, if you go beyond hell, then as you go upward, you will only have the directness and fineness of God's true path, His qualities, actions, peace, and tranquility. You will have the directness and fineness of these forms of justice, and there will be no differences of race, caste, relationships, family ties, brothers, 'I' and 'you', parent, or child. If you have these differences, their fire will burn you. It is these differences that burn together as the fire of the vilest hell.

The bridge that has been built over these fires is the bridge of Allah's justice, grace (rahmat), and absolute faith (īmān). You should walk on this bridge having realized the mizān trās. You should surrender to God, immerse yourself in God (baqā'), and annihilate everything other than God (*fanā'*). Then, it will be Allah who walks on the path. Then, you will not be burnt by the fires of hell; you will not perish in the canals. You will have the broad bridge of Allah's grace (*rahmat*) to walk upon.

You will hear shouts from below, "Brother!" "Sister!" "Mother!" They will try to pull you down by calling out, "Our religion! Our race! Come down here!" If you turn to listen to their sounds, you will fall. If you turn to one side satan and hell will be there, and on the other side will be illusion (*māyā*). From the side of illusion, the gales, winds, thunder, desires, and attachments will all strike against you. Four hundred trillion, ten thousand types of air will attack you. Blood ties, ghosts, demons, race, community, caste, religion, property, possessions, house, cattle, money, wealth, gold, silver, diamonds, gems, pride, praise, respect, rank, status, titles, ancestral pride, and honors will all attack you. If you turn toward them, they will knock you over with one blow. You will no longer see the subtle path, and you will be rolled around in the seven hells (*jahannam*).

These are the sounds that arise from hell. Each thought you hold in your mind will take a form and call to you. If you do not have the one-pointed focus, the one thought that comes from loving Allah and realizing the connection between Him and you; if you deviate from that focused awareness and concentration on Allah alone, you will fall. As soon as you turn even the slightest, if you deviate even a hair's breadth, you will fall.

Māyā will call out from one side, and satan and the angels (*malaks*) of hell will call out from the other side. Each of your thoughts will take form and call out to you. They will call out to you in the form of mother, father, race, brother, sister, money, wealth, gold, silver, house, and property. They will take four hundred trillion, ten thousand forms and emit sounds. They will rise up and call out to you, disguising themselves as light, as wisdom, and as divine wisdom (*gnānam*). There will be so many sounds calling out to you. The jinns, the fairies, and all other forms will try to entrance you.

If you do not offer yourself to God (*thānam*), if you do not surrender to Allah (*fanā'*) and disappear within Him (*baqā'*), then you will fall. It is Allah's path and only He walks on it. Then it will be a broad bridge. Otherwise, you will only see the path of base desires which is as narrow as one-seventh of a strand of hair. When you look at it, your glance will reduce it to still a narrower path, and you will not even be able to step foot on it. You will fall.

Therefore, to walk along this path you should surrender yourself to God and become *baqā'* (one who is totally immersed in God) and *fanā'* (one who has annihilated everything that is not God). First, offer yourself to God (*thānam*). Then concentrate and perceive only that path (*nithānam*). You should perceive only this. Block the ears that hear other sounds, the eyes that see other visions, the nose that smells other fragrances, and the mouth that speaks other words. At this time, only hold onto the speech that exists between Him and you, the sight between Him and you, the sound between Him and you, the smell between Him and you, and the taste between Him and you. Only hold onto the perceptions and conduct which exist between Him and you. With these perceptions, offer yourself to God (*thānam*), focus on Allah alone (*nithānam*), and walk with this justice and get to the other side.

However, you need even greater care and caution (*avathānam*) in order to proceed. If you do this and cross over the seven hells, then you will have divine wisdom (*gnānam*). You will meet Allah and speak to Him. At this point you have joined Him in His dwelling place, and you will speak and commune with Him. This is *Mi'rāj.*[2]

The base of the *mizān trās* is the place from which you will speak to Him. You will also see the *Rasūl* ⏀ at this place. The *Rasūl* ⏀ that you see in your dreams and your thoughts is not the true *Rasūl* ⏀. When you see the *Rasūl* ⏀, it will always be as a resplendent light. This is an entrusted eternal treasure. What you experience in your thoughts, desires, and sounds may appear to be the *Rasūl* ⏀, but what actually is this treasure? It is a light from God's power (*qudrat*) and grace (*rahmat*). You must think about this. It is only when you reflect upon this, that you can attain it. On this path, you have to safeguard this one treasure, you have to walk in this one manner, and you have to strive very hard.

Every second, we have to realize that our life has a limit. Our life is like a bubble in the water. When air becomes trapped within water, the bubbles rise to the surface. The bubbles do not last very long; they burst as soon as they reach the surface. Our life in this world is just like this. If we are hit by a stone, we could lose our life in a second. If we become dizzy and fall, we could die. We can lose our life while drinking water or even as we are eagerly putting food into our mouth. We could die when we are coming, going, standing, drinking, sitting, or sleeping. We do not know at what second we will reach the limit of our life.

We should not think that we are going to live forever. You should be ready to leave at any moment. Love God and His words at all times. Be ready at all times. Make yourself ready before you go to sleep. Prepare your prayers before you go to pray. Get ready for death before you die. Before your life comes to an end, understand what life is and live

---

2. The night journey of Prophet Muhammad ⏀ through the heavens, said to have taken place in the twelfth year of the Prophet's mission, on the twenty-seventh day of the month of *Rajab.*

accordingly. This is what you must do.

First, it is your duty to complete whatever you have to do. You cannot put the shroud of death (*kafan*) on yourself at the end; put it on at the beginning. You cannot bury yourself after you have died; prepare your burial before you die. You cannot judge yourself later on; make the judgment on yourself before that. Do not think that judgment day will come later; understand and make your own judgment. Before you die, you should understand what kind of house belongs to you. Understand these matters. With understanding, complete the work that has to be done, and having done that work, be ready at all times. Then your journey will be easy.

Do not decide to do things later on, saying, "I'll do it tomorrow" or "I'll do it later on." That is a way of saying you will not do it. It means that you no longer desire to complete the task and it will not be done. Finish each task at each second, on each day. Just complete it in some way. This is how you will see completion in your life. When you say, "Later" or "Tomorrow," it is the same as saying, "No." If you do not finish tasks that have to be done each day, it means that you cannot finish them. You are refusing to do them. Your yearning to do them no longer exists. You should understand this. We should understand this. As long as we do not realize this search and strive for it with every breath, we will not know our house, our own state. What kind of a house do we live in now? This can be understood from our qualities, actions, conduct, our inner heart (*qalb*), and mind. This must be understood.

I do not know what else to say. I am a crazy man who has come here. Because of my craziness I have stayed here for the last twenty or so years. I thought that other people who are crazy, like me, would come here. I thought, "If other people contract the same craziness that I have, we could stay together as a group." But to the extent that I can see, only

about ten or twelve people are acquiring this craziness little
by little. When I look at the others, I see that some people
had this obsession earlier, but it changed. The intellect took
over and they now have an intellectual craziness, not the real
obsession that we have. Very few people have the real
obsession that I have. However, this total craziness of a fool
is developing in a few people. God has provided this explanation. He has said, "One who perceives Me with complete
trust will be a fool in this world. He will appear to be completely crazy. Such a person has only one obsession. He is
crazy for divine wisdom (*gnānam*), he is crazy for Me." Such a
person gives up the experiences of the world and falls into
this craziness. Why does he do this? People will tell him,
"Look at everyone else, they have the craziness of the intellect, but you have the craziness of a fool."

Only if one becomes such a fool will God become the
physician who supports and assists him. Only God can take
care of a person with this obsession. The world, hell, and
satan can take care of intellectual craziness. But who can take
care of one who has this craziness? Only God can. He is the
only physician.

The total obsession that I have has developed to a small
extent in a few people, but the intellectual craziness has
taken over many people. Even those who initially had this
total craziness dwindled away as their intellect grew and
developed. Some of them have left and others are beginning
to leave.

If one considers himself to be a wise man, he will not
stay with fools. He will say, "That crazy man is blabbering
foolishly," and walk away. So-called wise people will run
away. Only crazy people will stay here and listen. Those
who had the total craziness earlier and developed intellectual
craziness will also leave. That is fine. Only those who have
this total craziness will try to stay here. They will try to

become fools who are totally obsessed. They do this because they believe that when they attain this state of complete craziness, a conclusive cure will be provided.

Those who have intellectual craziness will go to several doctors and undergo treatments. They think they are better off than those with one obsession, because they undergo many different treatments and therefore there is a greater likelihood of being cured. It is difficult to search for the One Physician. This is the way things are today.

"God alone is sufficient." This is what I was told a hundred or a hundred and fifty years ago. The first words I was told were, "My son, come here, I will give you an explanation. You are in the world now. There could be many different kinds of actions or practices in this world. Find ways to escape from these. The fire of hunger exists within man, as well as the fires of arrogance, karma, and illusion (māyā), the fires of anger, sin, and fanaticism, the fires of blood ties, racial prejudice, and color prejudice, the fires of selfishness, jealousy, envy, and pride.

"You are journeying through these fires now. You have been sent forth to travel through the world. Since you must walk through these fires you should remember what I am telling you now. 'Be first in line for food.' On Allah's path, this means that in the place where Allah is, in that permissible (halāl) place, be first in line to receive His nourishment. 'But be last in line for war.' This is the war fought by the six armies of arrogance, karma, and illusion (māyā) and the three sons of illusion (tārahan, singhan, and sūran), along with the six armies of lust, anger, miserliness, attachment, fanaticism, and envy and the five armies of intoxication, craving, theft, murder, and falsehood. These armies and troops march forward. This is the world. You should stand first in line for food on the path of truth, but stand far behind these armies. Do not attempt to go ahead of them, or you will lose your head. This is the world. Everyone will run behind these armies. You need to run in the center. Allah's house is there. Run there, to the center of the inner heart (*qalb*). When everyone joins the stampede, you should run in the center. This is how it should be done.

"Everyone in the cities, all the armies, all the various fascinations, birth and death will keep running. You need to also run amidst them and conduct your life. When everyone runs, run amidst them. But when a person is running alone, inquire, find out why he is running. Do not join him blindly and run with him. That could be dangerous. When you run alone, ask, inquire, and find the path. Find the place where the true sheikh is, ask him, receive the map, and continue to ask as you go along the path. You have to ask for guidance as you proceed alone on God's path.

"Do not proceed without asking for guidance. And even if you do, do not go in front. If you race ahead saying, 'I, I,' then powerful demons and all the ghosts of the world will be there. They will drink your blood. Do not stay behind either. Many ghosts are there. The base desires, the five elements, blood ties, attachments, property, relations, religions, and races are all gathered there. All these ghosts will catch hold of you. The ghosts of wealth and hunger will come and catch you. If you lag behind, the ghosts will catch hold of you, and if you go in front demons will strike you and suck your blood.

"Therefore, neither lag behind nor go in front. Go on the right path, walk in the middle without deviating. Go along this path and offer yourself to God. Make certain that you die here, at the *mizān trās*, the scale of judgment and the scale of death, and that you see the *Rasūl* ☪ here. Judgment is in your own hands. Determine your own judgment by weighing the permissible and impermissible (*halāl* and *harām*), right and wrong (*khair* and *sharr*), justice and injustice. Weigh

them using Allah's judgment. Lay yourself down before the
headstone of "Bismillāhir-Rahmānir-Rahīm. In the name of God,
Most Merciful, Most Compassionate." You, yourself, must
make this board on which the kalimah³ is written. Plant
absolute faith (īmān) within yourself at this central place.
Establish true determination, and firmly place the seal of one
who has true faith (mu'min). Plant this board that signifies you
have died in Allah. Establish this kind of judgment. Die here,
within Allah; create for yourself the death of one with true
faith and plant that board.

"This is what you should do. Then you will see the
Rasūl ☻ at the foot of the mizān trās, and hell will be moved
far away from you. You will not see hell, and you will cross
the bridge. However, if you fail to see the Rasūl ☻ here,
then you will not cross this bridge which is sharper than a
sword and straighter than wisdom. This is the bridge of
judgment which is a grace beyond Allah's grace. You should
walk on such a bridge. Once you realize this, the bridge is
very broad, and you can walk across it without mishap. The
fire and the sounds from below will not pay attention to you
or catch you. The sounds will rise up from all four sides, but
you will have blocked your ears, and you will proceed
listening only to His sounds. If you do not become one of
pure faith (mu'min), if you do not see the Rasūl ☻ at the foot
of the mizān trās, then all your sounds will call out to you. If
you listen to these sounds and turn around, illusion (māyā)
will pull you down on one side and hell will push you over
on the other side. This is the world.

"On this bridge you have to offer yourself to Allah
(thānam), surrender to Allah, immerse yourself in Him (baqā'),

_____

3. The affirmation of faith—Lā ilāha ill-Allāhu: There is nothing
other than You, O God. Only You are Allah.

208 To Die Before Death

and annihilate everything but God (*fanā'*). You should only see the connection between Allah and you. If you walk in this state, the sounds from below will not reach your ears. If you offer yourself to Allah (*thānam*), concentrate on Allah alone (*nithānam*), and proceed with great care and caution on the path to Allah (*avathānam*), if you have this level of caution and concentration, then you will cross the bridge and reach Allah. You will commune directly with Allah. This is Mi'rāj. You will reach Allah and be in complete communion with Him, just as the *Rasūl* ﷺ communed with Him.

"You must think about this. Otherwise, the sounds that you carry with you will call out to you from under the bridge. If, however, you have died before this as one of pure faith (*mu'min*) and have seen the *Rasūl* ﷺ at the foot of the *mizān trās*, and if the board has been firmly planted, then you will have no further death, no suffering in hell, and no further birth. You have finished dying in that place and you have attained eternal life (*hayāt*). Nothing can touch you now. As one of pure faith you attained eternal life and a form (*sūrat*) of light. You will no longer be born again or die again, and hell will have been pushed far away from you.

"This is the path you have to take to cross over to the other side. You have to think about this and act accordingly." This is what my sheikh told me at that time.

"This is what the world is like. This is what you have to attain. This is what the paths are like. You should inquire and ask for guidance along the way." My sheikh told me many such words a long time ago. I remembered them now and so I conveyed them to you.

Children, please think about it. You must understand what kind of a path this is. I have told you the type of conduct and behavior you need, and you should conduct yourselves in this way.

Sometimes I think, "What is the use of my coming here?

Of what use has it been? What have I seen after coming
here? Considering what I see, I think I could have stayed
where I was, studied further, and moved on. This is what I
am thinking. All I do is shout here."

Divine knowledge (*'ilm*) is not what you have learned,
recited, or studied. A stone has to be struck if we want to
create fire. Similarly, divine knowledge can be obtained only
by tapping Allah; absolute faith (*īmān*) can be obtained only
by tapping the *Rasūl* ⌾; and wisdom or light can be obtained only by tapping the *Qutb* ⌾.

Therefore, to attain divine knowledge (*'ilm*) you begin
by tapping the sheikh. You should start by bringing your
inner heart (*qalb*) and beating it against the sheikh. You
should strike your inner heart against the sheikh and extract
either the grace or the meaning from there. Whatever you
bring to a sheikh, he will change it and return it to you.

Once a beggar came to the *Rasūl* ⌾ seeking help from
the poverty and many difficulties of his life. The *Rasūl* ⌾
told the beggar to give him all the money he had. The
beggar gave him one cent.[4]

The *Rasūl* ⌾ received it in one hand, transferred it to
the other hand, changed it, and returned it to the Arab,
saying, "This is the wealth of God. Take this wealth and start
a business with it." And the man became rich. Similarly, the
sheikh changes whatever you bring and returns it to you. If
you bring base desires, he will say, "That's fine," and return
them to you. If you give him goodness, he will exalt it and
give it to you. If you bring him baseness, he will magnify
that and give it to you. If you bring him goodness and intend
that, he will increase it for you; he will fulfill your intention.

---

4. From the story, "The Rasūlullāh ⌾, The Beggar, and the Penny,"
in the book *My Love You, My Children: 101 Stories for Children of All Ages* by
M. R. Bawa Muhaiyaddeen.

He will accept your intention in one hand, transfer it into the other, and return it to you. It is not his fault. He merely increases and returns to you what you brought to him. He will only give you the same intention you brought to him and return it in an increased amount. If it is bad then bad will increase, if it is good then goodness will increase in you. Whatever path you ask for, he will magnify that path for you. Therefore, it is not his fault.

Think about this. Think about what you have to beat against in order to learn divine knowledge (*'ilm*). The *Rasūl* ﷺ said, "Go even unto China to receive divine knowledge." One has to ponder why the *Rasūl* ﷺ carried the Qur'an in his hand, gave the Qur'an to you, and yet proceeded to tell you to go even unto China to learn *'ilm*. He also said that the wisdom obtained from a discourse of wisdom (*hadīth*) is more subtle and exalted than fifty times (*waqts*) of prayer. He told people to listen to words of wisdom (*hadīth*).

There is a great difference between what you do and what the *Rasūl* ﷺ spoke about. You should determine what it is that you have to beat against. In order to revive the life of the soul, one must beat against the sheikh and obtain the life of divine knowledge (*'ilm*). The sheikh is the one of grace and divine knowledge. You have to strike against that in order to obtain the wealth (*daulat*). Do not think that you have learned and studied everything. That is of no use.

Reflect on this. May God help you. *Āmīn*. Search for your wealth. Seek and understand how to cross the bridge and go to the other side.

A man who continues to put out his hand even when it gets slapped is a fool, and the man who beats such a man is also a fool. If I continue to tell you things, even though the words do not penetrate your ears, then I am a fool. If you come, sit here, and do not take in the words, if time after time you sit there and just look at me, then you are also fools. If the words enter you, then that will help you. Otherwise, you and I will be like the fool who kept putting his hand out to be beaten and the fool who kept on beating it. I am a fool for continuing to talk when you do not listen and you are fools for continuing to come here and not listening when I am talking. We are like the two fools who have come together. This is of no use. It is wasted work. The effort on both sides is wasted. This is foolishness.

If your inner hearts (qalbs) open up in the right way and the words enter inside, then they will be of help and assistance. Both you and I will benefit from this. Whatever you do, do it correctly. When you try to cure a disease, put together the right medicines, mix them together, and administer them to the patient. Then the illness will be cured. You have to reflect before you do anything. Āmīn. May God help you.

June 29, 1981

22

To Live As a Human Being

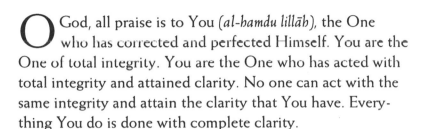

O God, all praise is to You (al-hamdu lillāh), the One who has corrected and perfected Himself. You are the One of total integrity. You are the One who has acted with total integrity and attained clarity. No one can act with the same integrity and attain the clarity that You have. Everything You do is done with complete clarity.

No matter how much we run about searching, only when we finally look with wisdom does everything become clear. As long as we do not have wisdom we cannot understand anything that You do; but with wisdom we can see everything clearly. Wisdom cuts through everything; huge jungles conjured up by our senses are pushed aside. When we try to look at You now, we see an enormous mountain. If we try to go around this mountain to find the path, we will not be able to circle it in an entire lifetime. However, if we focus intently, that mountain will split apart and a direct path will be created.

Precious jeweled lights, in this way, things that seem impossible to accomplish can be achieved when, with clarity, wisdom, high ideals, and good qualities, we help all other beings, clear ourselves, complete our work, and go forward. Without that awareness, wisdom, and analytic wisdom, our work is done without uniting with You. There are periods when we do not walk with You, and there are fools like me who do not dwell with You. It is such fools who do not understand Your actions that say, "What is God? Where is

God?" They praise themselves and find fault with You. Please forgive us for this.

You alone have the forbearance and capacity to forgive. Other than You, no one else will forgive our faults. Most people have even more anger than we do. We get angry with others, they get even more angry with us, and still others become infuriated with them. Forgiveness comes only from You. Only You have humility and because of that, You forgive. It is because You are filled with patience, contentment, trust, and praise (*sabūr, shakūr, tawakkul 'alallāh*, and *al-hamdu lillāh*), that You have the compassionate quality of forgiveness. Please give us the grace to acquire this quality. We need Your grace.

Precious jeweled lights of my eyes, in the name of God, the Most Compassionate, the Most Merciful (*Bismillāhir-Rahmānir-Rahīm*), that which appeared first rules and that which rules sustains. That which appeared and resplended became light; it dispels darkness and is the ruler. It sustains and takes care of everything that appears from within it, without expecting anything in return. This is God. He is the One of compassionate qualities who continues to do these duties within all lives. He is the Lord of the universes (*Rabbul-'ālamīn*), the Most Compassionate One (*ar-Rahmān*), the Most Merciful One (*ar-Rahīm*). It is this perfect treasure that we call God, or Allah. He has been given different names in different languages by the people of this world. The nine precious gems are called by various names according to their different colors and forms, but they are all gems. Some of them are more expensive than others; a jeweller can tell us their value, which are false and which are real. Different names have been given to the different gems, but we have really just named their colors. Similarly, within the kingdom of the One God, the First and Supreme Being, within His kingdom that encompasses the eight primary and eight intermediate compass points, we have focused on the different colors, hues, sounds, and languages and claim, "This is different, that is different."

My love you, my sisters, my brothers, my sons, daughters, grandsons, and granddaughters. I give my love to you, to all the American children, and to everyone in this world who are our brothers and sisters.

O Lord of the universes, that Most Compassionate One, that Protector, may You dispel our illnesses, poverty, and difficulties. O One of unfathomable grace, incomparable love, bestower of the undiminishing wealth of grace, please grant us the equanimity that brings peace. O God, the One who embraces us, all praise is to You (al-hamdu lillāh). May we praise You with contentment (shakūr), saying, "God is great! Allāhu Akbar!" May we give His sounds to Him and obtain bliss. May we give His qualities to Him and obtain great joy. May we give His happiness and His actions to Him and attain peace.

Jeweled lights of my eyes, when we plant a seedling, fertilize it, and water it, what do we experience as it grows— happiness and great joy. And who benefits from this? We do. When we plant a tree, water it, and fertilize it, it becomes beautiful, and when it is fully grown, the benefits are abundant. We experience the sweet taste of its fruits and feel happy. In the same way, we must cultivate and ripen God's ideals within us and give them to Him. Then He will be at peace and we can attain peace. We can realize this taste. We should do this in each aspect of our lives.

May all of us reflect, pray to God and His goodness, and bathe in wisdom. All of the children who are within my inner heart (qalb), may God embrace all of us in His heart and fill our lives with great bliss.

Precious children, there are many things we must reflect upon. Consider the following stories.

Once there was a pond with a fence nearby. A chameleon liked to jump on the fence and sit on one of its posts. There was also a frog that liked to jump onto the fence and warm itself in the heat of the sun. In the pond there were some turtles and other creatures too.

One day a man was passing by in his donkey cart. He was complaining, "My donkey does not move fast enough." He thought, "Maybe if I harness that chameleon and that frog to the cart, they might help the donkey move faster." And so he proceeded to catch the chameleon and the frog and hitch them to the cart.

If the man had continued with just the donkey, they would have slowly and eventually reached their destination. But now, the frog was trying to pull the cart toward the pond, and the chameleon was pulling it toward the fence. The two of them continued tugging in opposite directions, and it grew very late. The cart had not proceeded on the path at all but had only moved closer to the edge of the pond.

Similarly, like the pond in the orchard of wisdom within the inner heart (qalb) of God's grace (rahmat), countless things savor the taste of the fruits. Four hundred trillion, ten thousand spiritual qualities, energies (shaktis), and actions are there. They come there for their comfort and happiness, like the frog, the chameleon, and the insects that come to the pond. If we try to adopt their qualities, thinking that they will help us on our journey; if we let go of the path on which we were travelling and the things we have been carrying thus far, it will never work. If we do not at least make use of our first three levels of consciousness, feeling, awareness, and intellect, if we let go of these and do not establish and realize at least one of these states, and if instead we hold onto the monkey mind, desire, and hastiness, thinking we can harness them like a horse for our journey, we will not be able to continue on our way even for a single day. They will pull us here and there, and we will never be able to proceed on the path.

It is the mind that we have to discard. We should not trust it. The mind is like the frog that came out of the pond to dry itself in the sun, but as soon as it catches sight of people, it will jump back into the pond. The chameleon came there to eat worms and termites. Once it has eaten all it desires, it too will move away. If we pay attention to these animals, harness them to our cart and think that they will lead us, we will not be able to reach God. We will not be able to search for truth, and therefore, we will never be able to gain access to truth and proceed forward. We should reflect on this. If we take the mind with us and hold on to our desires and thoughts, it will be very difficult to reach the kingdom of God.

Jeweled lights of my eyes, there are several freight and passenger trains that travel to and from Philadelphia. The passenger train stops at each station for a minute and drops people off. The freight train stops at the appropriate stations for fifteen minutes to half an hour and delivers boxes of goods. Sometimes, the boxcars carrying the freight are unhitched and left behind at each stop. The train proceeds in this manner leaving each boxcar behind until it arrives at the final destination.

In the same way, in our life, we have to detach and leave behind each of the qualities that have hitched on to us. Each action has to be unloaded. We should only unload things at each station and not take on more things to pull.

There is not enough time to interrupt our work in this wasteful manner. Time moves on.

In our life, we have piled up hundreds of thousands of thoughts, fights, quarrels, and differences. It is impossible to tell how many things we have accumulated. Trying to extract and separate these from the ocean of illusion (*māyā*), which is our mind, is like trying to extract all the fish from the ocean. Their number is endless. In our lives, thoughts keep coming and coming to our mind, one after another. Some of the things that arise in the mind could kill us, like the bite of poisonous insects. So many kinds of things, both good and bad, enter the mind. Therefore, we have to continually sift through them, develop what is good, and watch the others closely.

Jeweled lights of my eyes, life is extremely subtle. Discovering or realizing this subtlety requires an even greater subtleness. Once this has been realized, implementing this awareness through action requires an even greater degree of subtlety. If we realize and understand this subtlety, then it will be easy to proceed.

Take for example a rapidly flowing river. It is indeed difficult to cross from one shore to the other, because the current flows so fast. We cannot cross in a boat, because the rapids will dash against it and wash it downstream. We have to find a 'special instructor', one who knows how to swim very well and can train others. Then he can take a heavy rope, fasten it on to this shore, take it across, and tie it firmly to the other shore. Additional ropes can then be added later when necessary. Several kinds of bridges can be constructed in this way, or the ropes can be used to pull a small ferry across. Then we can cross without the aid of anyone; we can use the rope to pull the boat along ourselves. Earlier, it was difficult. Now, we can easily go to and fro from this shore to the other.

In the same way, in this journey of ours, we are going from this world (*dunyā*) to the next world (*ākhirah*). We enter life and then proceed from this life to the hereafter. In order to proceed through life, in order to cross the ocean of illusion (*māyā*) and swim through its waves, we will have to struggle for a while. This is because we first have to discover the great subtlety. We have to discover certain things through a wise being who knows. We have to learn through that wisdom, that clarity, and those qualities. If we do, then it will become easier, and we will be able to carry our burdens to the other shore. In this way, each child must try to attain the clarity of wisdom that is necessary to discover and understand the subtlety of life. We should understand this truth, and with that wisdom, we should realize, sift, and separate everything.

At all times birth and death are hanging around our neck. They can occur very quickly. Within the blinking of an eye, there is time for either creation or destruction. If a crazy quality enters a man, he could die at once. However, if a good quality of wisdom comes, he could escape death and become one who lives again. Even when we are asleep, if the breath we inhale proceeds along the wrong course, we may die. It is possible that we may lie down and be unable to awaken. It is also possible for one to awaken, leave home, and never return. We do not know at which moment death may occur. We cannot trust death; it is not certain when it may come. The garland of death hangs around our neck playing with us. Yet, while death is around our neck, we are playing in this world. Death plays with us, and we play in the world thinking that we are going to live for a long time and accomplish so much.

Jeweled lights of my eyes, if a frog becomes arrogant and tries to catch and devour another frog, it does not stop to think that it should only eat it a little at a time, and if it exceeds this limit, the arrogant frog will die in the attempt. In its defense the frog being eaten will swell up when it is halfway down the arrogant frog's throat, and neither will be able to escape. They will both die. Similarly, we have to understand the world and proceed a little bit at a time. We have to defeat the world and go on, but we should proceed very slowly, gradually understanding one thing after another. If, instead, we say that the world is beautiful and try to grab hold of something and swallow it, we might encounter the same fate as the frog. In other words, two feet might be left sticking out of our mouth as the frog swells up within us.

I saw this happen at my farm in Paliayankulam. A big frog attempted to swallow another frog in the well and both died. When I saw it in the morning, the big frog had become so swollen that it weighed five pounds. We had to fish it out of the well and drain all the water.

In a similar manner, our thoughts kill us by attempting to swallow us. They are unable to let go of us, and we die in the process. Likewise, we also try to swallow each of our thoughts and die in the attempt. We must reflect on this.

Jeweled lights of my eyes, life can be very simple if we hold on to what is wise.

Is it not easy for a chameleon to climb a tree? It is very easy. But a man trying to climb a tree has to struggle and work hard. A snake coils itself around the tree and slides upward with ease. But a man cannot climb by sliding around and around the tree; he has to proceed upward in a fairly direct manner, holding on as he ascends. Therefore, it is more difficult for him.

Like the snake, the mind will catch hold of life and go around and around in circles, but wisdom will look straight ahead, pay attention, and proceed. In our life we simply have to hold on to what is wise and proceed upward in a direct manner. The monkey of the mind will just dance in circles and laugh at everything it sees. That is why we have to reflect very deeply in our lives. This is how it is, my brother.

We should reflect upon each thing in a state of love. Our love should be fragrant. Our every word should bring sweetness to the heart and be tasty to the tongue. Our every gaze should bring peace and happiness to others. We should have the kind of embrace that draws all children to our hearts with love. We have nothing else to give others, only our heart. When we give our hearts, we emit that love. At once people's hunger will cease, and they will be filled with love, compassion, and a beautiful taste. We may not have water or food to give, we may be starving too, but we are not without love and compassion. As soon as we talk to others and give them love and compassion, their tiredness, sadness, and worry will leave them. Then we can offer them some water, and they can drink it and be refreshed.

In the same way, if you possess each quality of God, you will be able to give peace to every life. You will not say, "I don't have!" Instead you will say, "There is, there is! The completeness is here. The fullness, the plenitude, is here!" and you will bring comfort to all inner hearts (*qalbs*). Love is that fullness and plenitude. Compassion is a high ideal. Mercy causes the heart of a human being to melt. Therefore, having mercy and compassion toward other lives makes one's own heart melt. A melting heart shows that it is full of love. Each child should think about this.

There are so many varieties of fish that live in the

ocean. Some have electricity within them, some are very cold, and some are poisonous. Some fish have as much as four or five hundred volts of electric current. If they touch another fish, that fish dies. Like this, there are also many things within us. Electricity is within us and light is also within us. When certain bad things touch us, the electricity will strike them. But some evil things cannot be stopped by the electricity. There are many sections in our hearts. Among these are the qualities of trying to kill others and trying to defeat others. Because of these qualities, we bring sorrow and difficulties to others. However, we have to try to bring peace to all other lives, and to do that we first have to make our own inner heart (qalb) peaceful.

The four yugas are practically over. This is the Kali yuga.[1] Two hundred million years have passed by. During this time several wars have taken place. Each war has occurred out of desire for women, politics, positions, and titles, out of desire to capture other kingdoms, land, and wealth. The purānas show that the wars between kingdoms came about in this manner. Men fought and a king became a beggar and a beggar became a king. The world has continued in this way for a long time. These have been written down as purānas. A person was once a king and now he is a purāna, an ancient epic. They were written as stories or histories of men and now they are considered to be the stories or history of God. What these stories consist of, however, are battles caused by the desire for titles, attachments, wealth, and women. Now they are considered to be battles fought by gods.

For two hundred million years, wars have occurred over and over again. There has never been a time without war;

---

1. In Hinduism, there are four ages or eras of the world, each being shorter, darker, and less righteous than the previous one. The last, the present age, is the Kali yuga.

there has never been a time when one kingdom is not attempting to take over another kingdom. Now there are no more kingdoms, and we have come to the state of democracy. From a government by the people, we have come to a government by murder. This has taken over the world and is called socialism. Socialism is governing through murder, through burning, destroying, and killing others. One person after another is killed.

Historically, these changes have taken place in two hundred million years. More people have died than are alive in the world today. Millions of people died in wars and their corpses fill the earth. The dead cattle, donkeys, horses, monkeys, and human beings outnumber the living. Very few lives are left, but the wars have not ended. The wars will not end until this *yuga* comes to an end. What will happen in the next *yuga*? What will we see at the end of this? Nothing. Man will have destroyed himself. He has already destroyed and devoured so many animals. There is no goodness left. Cities have become jungles and jungles have become cities. Cemeteries have become cities and cities have become cemeteries. Land has become ocean and ocean has become land. Humans have turned to beasts and beasts have become like humans. Monkeys have begun to be dressed in clothes and humans have discarded their clothes and run naked in the woods. Many, many kinds of changes have taken place. Monkeys from the jungle have come into the cities to perform in the circus and to do other kinds of work, while the human-monkeys have discarded everything and retreated into the woods to find peace. Everything has changed. Everything is different and strange.

When we look at this and reflect upon it, we realize how much there is yet to learn. These events are not the real wars; all the battles are within oneself. What we see around us is not the city; all the cities are within us. This is not heaven; heaven is within us. This is not hell; hell is only within us. These are not our relatives; our relatives are within us in the form of love. The qualities born of compassion are our true relatives. The people around us are not our blood ties. Our true blood ties are the trust, equanimity, and peace that fill compassion and flow out of it. These qualities are what are truly connected to the heart. They are the form of love.

We have to look at each aspect of our life in this way. If we open up each thing and look, we will see how much beauty lies there. When a flower opens up, it reveals its fragrance and its beauty. In the same way, when we attain clarity in each situation, the beauty, fragrance, and qualities that arise will bring such bliss. This beauty will be seen in the face. We should look at each enemy or person we dislike in the same way. When we look at a little child, we should see the same beauty. When we look at a very big person, that beauty is there. When we see a youth, that beauty is there. We should ponder and reflect upon each thing.

There is no use in talking. Speech is useless. Only the bliss and peace that flows out of the inner heart like the fragrance flows out of the flower, only this will bring peace. Only this is fragrant. This will emerge from the inner heart of every child.

If we want to have peace, help others attain peace, and destroy the demons of difficulties and losses in this world, then we ourselves have to attain peace. We have to make our hearts peaceful and then manifest it on the outside.

If there is water in the pond, it is easy to drink. But if there is no water in the pond, how can we drink? We will not go there anymore. Similarly, only if peace exists in our hearts will others come and attain peace. They can take from our hearts and benefit from it. If we have not found equanimity, peace, and tranquility, how can we give it to others? Like a pond without water, we will have nothing to give.

We have to develop compassion, love, benevolence, generosity, and mercy within us and demonstrate it to others. Our inner hearts are very small. God is enormous. He is in everything that moves and everything that does not move. But the place in which He dwells is as small as an atom within an atom, a particle within a particle. As our wisdom grows and increases, our inner heart will become smaller and smaller. As it gets smaller and smaller its light and resplendence will increase. If we become small that light, that perfection, will become big. If we become big, that will become small. This is the way it is. We have to think about this.

Precious children, each one of you, please look at your hearts. You should search for the qualities and inherent characteristics of God. That is our wealth. That is our life's wealth, the perfect treasure. We should hold on to this and attain peace. We are struggling like travellers without water in a desert. Today this is the way it is in a heart without love, in a heart without compassion, in a world without mercy. In this hell-like earth, where man lives without unity and peace, we are wandering about searching for truth. A few people are searching for truth and goodness in this world, and because of this search they encounter many difficulties. They encounter more bad than good, but they have to continue to search for the truth.

Precious children, each child must reflect and accept what is good. My love and greetings (salāms) to all of you. Please forgive my faults. I may have spoken with or without knowing and with or without realizing. I ask forgiveness for these faults. Jeweled lights of my eyes, if there is anything wrong with what I have said, please forgive me. We should always search for and go toward what is good. God must bestow His grace and we should do our work. Presently, we are developing within us things that will burn us. The mind, desire, and thoughts are the things that will torture and kill us. The illnesses that will cause us difficulty are living with us. They are pricking us and causing pain. We should remove these thorns. These are the qualities we retain because of our lack of realization. If we remove these qualities, our illnesses will be cured and we will have peace. We must think about this.

Jeweled lights of my eyes, we need patience, contentment, trust in God, and the ability to praise God in all situations. Patience is very important in our lives. We also need faith, certitude, and proper conduct. Our death will certainly come some day. Some day we will have judgment. Some day, depending on what we have searched for and acquired, we will receive either heaven or hell. We will receive a decision or a judgment.

No matter how long we may live, the world we live in does not belong to us; neither does the place we dwell in belong to us. This is merely a school where we have come to study about birth and death, good and evil, heaven and hell, man and God, human beings (insān) and beasts (hayawāns), creation and death, beauty and ugliness, and happiness and sorrow. We have to take account of all this and learn. Within this learning, we should understand what is what. We should search within this to understand good and bad, birth and death. We should assess all these things.

It is through this learning that we should become people of pure faith (mu'mins) and die before death. We should study hard so that we die as ones with pure faith and not as ignorant satans or as animals. Before the angels Munkar and Nakīr ☺ ask the questions in the grave, we should have developed the goodness that can give the answers. We should adopt each quality of God, understand it, work at it, cultivate it, and receive the benefit from it.

Then from these qualities, the answers can be given to the
angels who write down the good and the bad that you do.
Give them the sharp point of your wisdom, give them
absolute faith (*īmān*), wisdom, and clarity to write with. You
will be awakened on the Day of Resurrection, but if we die
before death, all the questioning will be over, and we will
have understood death and everything else. We should die
as ones with pure faith before our physical death, and then
we will go to a place where we cannot die. We will put to
death the place where we were born and the place where we
will die and depart to a place of deathlessness. From this
place we will speak to God. The questioning about good and
bad will then be completed.

We have come here to gather these answers. We
emerged from God as light and we came here to the earth as
human beings. When we die, we leave as a corpse. When we
return to Him, we should be a fragrance; if we die a physical
death, we are just a corpse. We should change this form. We
came from there as a light. We came to the earth and
changed into Adam, or man. Now we have to become true
human beings with wisdom. In our lifetime, we have to
transform into beings filled with the grace of God. We have
to learn what we came here to learn, we have to extract this
learning from the world and leave as people with pure faith
(*mu'mins*). One who has pure faith is a being of perfect purity
and resplendence. When we accomplish this and go there,
we will be God's son, a being with resplendent fragrance.
We will be with our Father, and we can attain His kingdom.

We should work hard to attain this state. This is what
we came here to learn. If we investigate and study properly,
then we can return to our Father. This is the school that
educates us and prepares us to return to our Father. There are
many experiences within this life. We came here only to
study all these things. Here we can discover the ideals of life,

understand the secrets of the fourteen realms, and study the eighteen thousand universes. This is what we came here for. We should at least do this a little at a time. We should at least touch a drop of it and say, "He is good, He is good, I too must become good."

We should touch at least one drop of it and pray to the Lone One who rules and sustains (Allāhu ta'ālā Nāyan). What is true prayer? His actions, His qualities, His conduct, His worship, and His sound should go and pray to Him. That is worship ('ibādat). We must dispel the part that is us, and that which is Him must pray to Him.

A flower can only give its own fragrance. Is this not so? The fragrance of a flower is what the flower should give. Only a jasmine can give the fragrance of a jasmine. The fragrance of Allah has to be given only by Allah—that is true prayer. Other than this fragrance, the smell of man and the stench of the base desires cannot reach that state. When the fragrance of the good thoughts of Allah, His ninety-nine powers (wilāyāt) and three thousand benevolent qualities emanate from our inner heart—that is prayer. That fragrance will reach Him.

I give you my love, jeweled lights of my eyes. Each child must think of this. We must reflect on this and make the effort to study and attain the beautiful grace and wealth of God (rahmat). Then we can attain victory of life. Āmīn. Āmīn.

As-salāmu 'alaikum wa rahmatullāhi wa barakātuhu kulluhu.

March 17, 1985

23

Prayer and Forgiveness

My love you. I seek refuge in God from the evils of satan, the rejected one *(A'ūdhu billāhi minash-shaitānir-rajīm.)* In the name of God, Most Merciful, Most Compassionate. *(Bismillāhir-Rahmānir-Rahīm.)* May we give all praise and adoration to the One God, who is infinite grace, incomparable love, and the bestower of the undiminishing wealth of grace. *Āmīn.*

May He bless us with His beneficent qualities, His actions, His conduct, His truth, and His qualities of patience, contentment, trust in God, and praise of God. May He bestow these upon us. *Āmīn.* May He bless us with His flawless thoughts and actions, His pure conduct and compassionate grace. May He bestow upon us all of His qualities. May He grant us His munificent grace and bless us with the wealth of all three worlds,[1] His precious qualities, and the wealth of those qualities.

O Most Exalted One, please bestow Your beneficence upon us! Grant us Your grace by teaching us Your three thousand gracious characteristics. Show us how to proceed using these qualities. Please bestow Your grace upon us and give us the certitude to conduct our lives with complete trust and surrender to You *(tawakkul).* *Āmīn.* Please open the direct

---

1. The three worlds refer to the following three Arabic terms: *awwal*—the time of creation when the soul becomes surrounded by form; *dunyā*—this world of physical existence; *ākhirah*—the hereafter.

path that connects our soul with You and guide us through this path without ever letting go of our hand. May You do this. *Āmīn*.

Without forsaking us, now or in the future, may You always embrace us. Please keep us under Your protection now and always at Your divine feet. Protect us until we come right up to where You dwell and keep us under Your protection. Please grant us Your grace in this way. *Āmīn*.

Just as You brought peace to Your prophets, illumined beings, and divinely wise ones (*nabīs, olis,* and *qutbs*), amidst the sorrow, joy, and trouble inflicted on them by the people of the world, just as You guided them to a state without personal difficulty, like this O Allah, even though we are faced with so much loss and difficulty in the world, even though people cause us so much grief, anguish, and torment of mind, may You give us fortitude, courage, certitude, and good conduct and embrace us. May You show us the path to peace and grant us Your grace.

When things are pressing in on us and tormenting us, please help us so that we will not dwell upon those things. Instead, help us to stay in Your state of love and find happiness and peace. Give us the steadfastness to do this. Give us the wealth of the good qualities of peace, unity, tranquility, honesty, and sincerity. May You give us these qualities and true wisdom. *Āmīn. Āmīn. Āmīn.*

Precious children, jeweled lights of my eyes, my love you, my daughters and sons. My love you, my sisters and brothers. My love you, my grandsons and granddaughters. My love you. May our Father sustain all of us. May He forgive all our faults and take us back to Him. May He correct our lives, lead us on the straight path, forgive us our sins, gather us into His beneficent qualities and His beautiful actions, and bestow His grace upon us. May He forgive us for everything and bless us with His pure treasures. May we praise that Benevolent One every minute and every second of the day. May we love Him every second of the day without forgetting Him in our innermost hearts (qalbs). May we remember Him always.

Precious jeweled lights of my eyes, this is how you must place your faith in Him. With every breath, ask Him for forgiveness. With every breath, think of Him, remember Him, and pray to Him. Prayer and His forgiveness will be the treasures that belong to us. Forgiveness will rid us of the faults we have committed; they will be erased. In our life, forgiveness is the eraser. It is the eraser that will wipe away the sins we have committed. We have to shape and fashion that eraser with our own hands and then hand it over to God, so that He may wipe away our faults.

Prayer is our treasure of paradise. Intending God and worshiping Him is the treasure of paradise. Our qualities are the arms that embrace our brethren. Our qualities will change the tiredness and sorrow in the hearts of our brothers and sisters. Love, wisdom, and good qualities are the wealth that can dispel the darkness in their hearts. They will be the wealth of love. When this wealth of love and its compassion are bestowed on others, their anxiety, fatigue, and agitation will be changed. This can be accomplished only through good qualities. We must develop these qualities within ourselves. We must fashion the qualities of God within, and with every breath, we must ask for forgiveness.

In everything we seek and in all things we strive for, there may be faults, so we must ask for forgiveness. We must take the eraser of forgiveness, fashion it with each breath, and make it strong enough so that God may erase away all our sins. The eraser of forgiveness is the only thing that can wipe away our sins. Therefore, fashion that, create that, within each breath. We have to develop the intention and the breath necessary for prayer, meditation, worship, and service ('*ibādat*). We have to create it, develop it, and give it into God's hands. That will be the paradise in our lives. Then we will attain paradise.

In every breath, we must establish these two, prayer and forgiveness, and hand them to God. We should also develop God's qualities in order to dispel the sorrow, grief, and darkness in the hearts of our brethren in the world. We should take His qualities and bring about brotherly unity. But we continue to be those who sin with every thought, every look, and every intention. Sins are swarming within us, overwhelming us. Therefore, with every breath, we must give this eraser of forgiveness into God's hands, so that He may erase our sins. It is through the prayer we perform with each breath that we attain paradise. This is the straight path to our Father's kingdom. We must do this. On the right is paradise, on the left is forgiveness.

A heart of perfect purity is one which has been cleared and within which His qualities have developed. We must utilize this pure heart to do things that benefit others and thereby attain our own fulfillment. This is the way to show God, the Lone One who sustains and protects (*Allāhu ta'ālā Nāyan*), that we have reached a state of completion. We must attain victory in this manner.

May we reflect on this. My love you. Please, every one of you, think about this. There will be a direct inquiry on the Day of Judgment. Face to face, we will be asked questions. If we establish this pure state within us, it will be the medicine, the correct answer to the questioning that will determine the final decision. When we are asked the questions, this state will be the beautiful response. Forgiveness, prayer, and God's qualities are what will bring us peace. May we reflect on this.

Each child has to fashion these inside his heart. If you succeed in doing this, only good will come to you and this will bring you peace. May we reflect on this. My love you, precious children, jeweled lights of my eyes. May Allah,

Almighty God, give us His grace and His blessing. And may He make it strong within us. *Āmīn.*

July 8, 1984

GLOSSARY

GLOSSARY

⸻❦⸻

The following traditional supplications in Arabic calligraphy are
used throughout the text:

⟦✦⟧ or (Sal.) following the Prophet Muhammad or *Rasūlullāh*
stands for *sallallāhu 'alaihi wa sallam*, blessings and peace be upon
him.

⟦✦⟧ or (A.S.) following the name of a prophet or an angel
stands for *'alaihis-salām*, peace be upon him.

⟦✦⟧ or (Ral.) following the name of a companion of the
Prophet Muhammad, a saint, or *khalīf* stands for *radiyallāhu 'anhu* or
'anhā, may Allah be pleased with him or her.

(A) Indicates an Arabic word

(T) Indicates a Tamil word

Abū Bakr as-Siddīq ⟦✦⟧ (A) Abū Bakr, "the truthful, the veracious," was
a title given to Abū Bakr ⟦✦⟧ by Muhammad ⟦✦⟧. He was a
companion of the Prophet ⟦✦⟧ and was the first caliph. He governed
for two years and died on August 22, 634 A.D. Abū Bakr ⟦✦⟧ was
the father of 'Ā'ishah ⟦✦⟧, a wife of the Prophet ⟦✦⟧.

ahādīth (A) (sing. *hadīth*) In Islam, authenticated statements relating to
the deeds and utterances of the Prophet Muhammad ⟦✦⟧ and his
companions. *See also* hadīth.

aham (T) The heart; the beauty of the heart.

ahamad (T & A) A Tamil variant of an Arabic word. The state of the
heart, the *qalb*, or *aham*. Ahamad is the heart of Muhammad ⟦✦⟧. The
beauty of the heart (*aham*) is the beauty of the countenance (*muham*
(T), *muhaiyyan* (A)) of Muhammad ⟦✦⟧. That is the beauty of Allah's
qualities. This is not merely a name that has been given. It is a
name that comes from within the ocean of divine knowledge
(*bahrul-'ilm*). Allah is the One who is worthy of the praise of the
heart (*qalb*). Lit. most praiseworthy.

'Ā'ishah Nāyahi ⟦✦⟧ (A) The wife of Prophet Muhammad ⟦✦⟧,
daughter of Abū Bakr ⟦✦⟧. The Honored Lady 'Ā'ishah ⟦✦⟧ was

237

known as *Ummul-Mu'minīn*, the Mother of the true believers. She died in Medina in 58 A.H., 678 A.D. at the age of sixty-seven.

aiyō (T) An exclamatory expression, "Oh no!"

ākhirah (A) The hereafter; the next world; the kingdom of God.

'ālam (A) (pl. *'ālamīn*) A world; cosmos; universe.

al-hamdu lillāh (A) All praise is to God. Allah is the glory and greatness that deserves all praise. "You are the One responsible for the appearance of all creations. Whatever appears, whatever disappears, whatever receives benefit or loss—all is Yours. I have surrendered everything into Your hands. I remain with hands outstretched, spread out, empty, and helpless. Whatever is happening and whatever is going to happen is all Yours."

A-L-H-M-D (A) The five letters, *alif, lām, mīm, hā', dāl* of the Arabic alphabet, which constitute the heart, become transformed in the heart of a true human being into *alhmd*, or *al-hamd*, the praise of Allah. *Alif* (l) represents Allah, the One God; *lām* (ل) represents the *Nūr*, the light of wisdom; *mīm* (م) represents Muhammad ☺, Allah's eternal Messenger; *hā'* (ح) represents the physical body; and *dāl* (د) represents the *dunyā*, or world.

alif (A) The first letter of the Arabic alphabet (l). To the transformed man of wisdom, the *alif* represents Allah, the One.

'ālim(s) (A) Learned ones. *See also 'ulamā'*.

Allah or *Allāhu* (A) God; the One of infinite grace and incomparable love; the One who gives of His undiminishing wealth of grace; the One who is beyond comparison or example; the Eternal, Effulgent One; the One of overpowering effulgence.

Allāhu Akbar (A) God is great!

Allāhu ta'ālā (A) God Almighty; God is the Highest. *Allāhu*: the beautiful undiminishing One. *Ta'ālā*: the One who exists in all lives in a state of humility and exaltedness.

Allāhu ta'ālā Nāyan (A & T) God is the Lord above all. *Allāhu*: (A) Almighty God. *Ta'ālā*: (A) the One who exists in all lives in a state of humility and exaltedness. *Nāyan*: (T) the Ruler who protects and sustains.

ambiyā' (A) (sing. *nabī*) Prophets.

Āmīn (A) So be it. May He make this complete; may it be so.

amīr (A) Prince; leader.

ammārah (A) See *nafs*.

ānmā (A) The spirit or essence of the elements; one of the three components of life (*ānmā, āvi, rūh*).

annam (T) The food; the nourishment (*rizq*) of all creations.

'arsh (A) The throne of God; the plenitude from which God rules; the station located on the crown of the head, which is the throne that can bear the weight of Allah. Allah is so heavy that we cannot carry the load with our hands or legs. The *'arsh* is the only part of man that can support Allah.

arwāh (A) (sing. *rūh*) Souls, the light rays of God.

ash-hadu al-lā ilāha ill-Allāh wahdahu lā sharīka lah, wa ash-hadu anna Muhammadan 'abduhu wa rasūluh (A) I witness (testify) that there is no god except the One God and Muhammad is the Messenger of God.

as-salāmu 'alaikum (A) May the peace and peaceful   s of Allah be upon us. This is the greeting of love. *As-salāmu alaikum, wa 'alaikumus-salām*. One heart embraces the other with love and greets it with respect and honor. Both hearts are one. In reply, *wa 'alaikumus-salām* means: May the peace and peacefulness of Allah be upon you also.

as-salāmu 'alaikum wa rahmatullāhi wa barakātuhu kulluhu (A) May all the peace, the beneficence, and the blessings of God be upon you.

astaghfirullāhal-'azīm (A) O Allah, forgive all our faults and correct us. I seek forgiveness from Allah, the Supreme.

asura(s) (T) Demon; a demon clan in Hindu mythology.

āthi (T) Primal beginning; the period after *anāthi*; the time when the Qutb (the wisdom which explains the truth of God) and the *Nūr* (the plenitude of the light of Allah) manifested within Allah; the time of the dawning of the light; the world of grace where the unmanifested begins to manifest in the form of resonance. In contrast to *awwal*, when the creations became manifest in form, *āthi* is the time when the first sound or vibration emerged.

a'ūdhu billāhi minash-shaitānir-rajīm (A) I seek refuge in God from the evils of the accursed satan. Please annihilate satan from within me. Eliminate him from within me and burn him up. *Minal* (T) is the fire of the resplendent light that comes like lightning. In the same way that lightning strikes, burn him away from me. Burn satan who is the enemy to the children of Adam ☮. He is the one who has separated us from You, O God. Please prevent that enemy from coming and mingling within us. Prevent him from coming once again into our midst, and take us back to You.

auliyā' (A) (sing. *walī*) The favorites of God; those who are near to God; referring to holy ones of Islam.

avathānam (T) Concentration; attentiveness.

āvi (T) The pure vapor or pure spirit; one of the three components of life (*ānmā, āvi, rūh*).

awwal (A) The time of the creation of forms; the stage at which the soul became surrounded by form and each creation took shape; the stage at which the souls of the six kinds of lives (earth life, fire life, water life, air life, ether life, and light life) were placed in their respective forms. Allah created these forms and then placed that entrusted treasure which is the soul within those forms.

āyat(s) (A) A verse in the Qur'an; a sign or miracle.

Badushāh (Persian) Ruler; Primal Emperor.

bahrul-'ilm (A) The ocean of divine knowledge.

baqā' (A) The subsistence of God. *See also fanā' wa baqā'.*

barzakhul-'ālam (A) The sphere or realm between this world and the hereafter. That universe (*'ālam*) contains the wisdom of Allah's grace (*rahmat hikmat*), His essence (*dhāt*). The 124,000 prophets dwell in that place. It is called a place of mystery, that exists between Allah and the world. That place is in the heart (*qalb*). The soul resides there and is concealed. When the soul is raised from the grave all the parts of the body start to work again. The twenty-eight letters of the body are brought back to life. Questions are asked and the eyes, ears, nose, and all the twenty-eight letters will say what each one did. They give evidence to what they did. Once its questioning is over, the soul goes to the hereafter (*ākhirah*), to Allah. The place where the soul is contained in the body between the time of death and the time it is raised from the grave is known as *barzakhul-'ālam*.

Bismillāhir-Rahmānir-Rahīm (A) In the name of God, Most Merciful, Most Compassionate.
  Bismillāh: Allah, the first and the last; the One with a beginning and without a beginning. He is the One who is the cause for creation and for the absence of creation, the cause for the beginning and for the beginningless. He is the One who is

completeness.

Ar-Rahmān: He is the King, the Compassionate One, and the Beneficent One. He is the One who protects all creations and gives them nourishment. He looks after them, gives them love, takes them unto Himself, and comforts them. He gives them food, houses, property, and everything within Himself. He holds His creations within Himself and protects them. He is the One who reigns with justice.

Ar-Rahīm: He is the One who redeems, the One who protects us from evil, the One who preserves and confers eternal bliss. No matter what we may do, He has the quality of forgiving us and accepting us back. He is the Tolerant One who forgives all the faults we have committed. He is the Savior. On the Day of Judgment, on the Day of Inquiry, and on all days since the beginning, He protects and brings His creations back unto Himself.

Bismin (A) A shortened form of *Bismillahir-Rahmānir-Rahīm* which means: In the name of God, Most Merciful, Most Compassionate.

Bismin kāi (A & T) The *Bismin kāi* is a piece of flesh, a small node on the outer surface of the right side of the heart, near the lungs. It is called a piece of flesh and within it is a point, a power, a place where the light dwells. It is God's house. He placed wisdom, the *alif,* the *qutbiyyat* (the sixth level of consciousness which explains the truth of God), and everything else within it. Within it is the explanation that makes you remember things.

The *Bismin kāi* is indestructible. It can never be destroyed by anything. It is through this point that we are raised up from the grave on the Day of Questioning (*Qiyāmah*). All the good and bad that we have done is within that point, and it will be raised up and questioned.

The *Bismin kāi* exists in humans as well as in animals. If the one who performs the *qurbān* (the ritual slaughter of animals to make them permissible to eat) has a clear heart and absolute faith (*īmān*), then no blood will stay within the *Bismin kāi* of the animal he slaughters.

This point is the place where the *dhikr* goes and stays. (*Dhikr* is the constant remembrance of God, the constant recitation of *Lā ilāha ill-Allāhu:* There is nothing other than You, O God. Only God exists.) God has built this in a subtle way for man to pray and dwell with God. Going there and worshiping there is the only true prayer.

Dastagīr (Persian) Lord; the helping hand.

daulat (A) The wealth of the grace of Allah. The wealth of Allah is the wealth of divine knowledge (*'ilm*) and the wealth of perfect *imān* (absolute faith, certitude, and determination). Lit. power or state of rulership.

dēva(s) (T) Celestial being.

dhāt (A) The essence of God; His treasury; His wealth of purity; His grace.

dhikr (A) The remembrance of God. It is a common name given to certain words in praise of God. Of the many *dhikrs*, the most exalted *dhikr* is to say, "*Lā ilāha ill-Allāhu*—There is nothing other than You, O God. Only You are Allah." All the others relate to His actions (*wilāyāt*), but this *dhikr* points to Him and to Him alone. *See also kalimah; Lā ilāha ill-Allāhu.*

dīnul-Islām (A) The faith of surrender to the will of Allah.

du'ā' (A) A prayer of supplication.

dunyā (A) The earth-world in which we live; the world of physical existence; the darkness which separated from Allah at the time when the light of the *Nūr Muhammad* manifested from within Allah.

fanā' (A) The annihilation of the ego, or false self. *See fanā' wa baqā'.*

fanā' wa baqā' (A) The two halves of the *kalimah*: If I am there God is not; if God is there I am not. The annihilation of self, leading to the subsistence of God.

fard (A) (pl. *furūd*) An obligatory duty. *See also furūd.*

Fātimah ☺ (A) Daughter of Muhammad ☺ by his first wife, Khadījah ☺. She married Muhammad's ☺ cousin, 'Alī ☺, by whom she had three sons, Hasan ☺, Husain ☺, and Muhsin. The latter died in infancy. From the two former are descended the posterity of the Prophet ☺, known as *sayyids*. Fātimah ☺ died six months after her father. She is spoken of by her father as one of the four perfect women and is called *al-Batūl*, the Virgin, and Fātimah Zuhrā, the beautiful Fātimah.

fikr (A) Contemplation; meditation; concentration on God.

Furqān (A) Islam. This is the fourth step of spiritual ascendance, the teachings revealed to Moses ☺ and Muhammad ☺. When asked, Bawa Muhaiyaddeen included Judaism in this step, explaining that these two religions are like two brothers decending from one father, Abraham ☺. Literally, *Furqān* is the "criterion" which distinguishes

between good and evil, right and wrong, lawful and unlawful, truth
and illusion.

The inner form of man (*sūratul-insān*) is made up of the four
religions. First is Hinduism (*Zabūr*), the religion in which forms are
created. In the human body, Hinduism relates to the area below the
waist. Second is Fire Worship (*Jabrāt*) which relates to hunger,
disease, and old age and is in the area of the stomach. Third is
Christianity (*Injīl*). This is the region of the chest which is filled
with thoughts, emotions, spirits, and vapors. Fourth is *Furqān*, which
corresponds to the head and the seven openings (two eyes, two
ears, two nostrils, and one mouth), through which man receives
explanations.

furūd (A) (sing. *fard*) Obligatory duties. The five *furūd* refer to the five
pillars of Islam: *ash-shahādah* (witnessing that none is God except
Allah and Muhammad is His Messenger), prayer, charity, fasting,
and holy pilgrimage (*hajj*).

Allah has also given us six inner *furūd*, which the Sufis have
explained: 1) If you go deep into Allah with the certitude of
unwavering faith, you will see that within this eye of yours is an
inner eye which can gaze upon Allah. 2) Within this nostril is a
piece of flesh which can smell the fragrance of Allah. 3) Within this
ear is a piece of flesh which can hear the sounds of Allah. 4) Within
this tongue is a piece of flesh which can taste the beauty and the
divine knowledge of Allah and know the taste of His wealth.
5) Within this tongue is also a voice which converses with Him and
recites His remembrance in a state of total absorption. 6) And
within this innermost heart is a piece of flesh where the eighteen
thousand unverses, the heavens, and His kingdom are found. And
there the angels, the heavenly beings, prophets, and lights of Allah
prostrate before Him.

gnānam (T) Divine luminous wisdom. If a person can throw away all
the worldly treasures and take within him only the treasure called
Allah and His qualities and actions, His conduct and behavior, if he
makes Allah the only treasure and completeness for him—that is
the state of *gnānam*.

gnāni(s) (T) A gnostic; one who has divine wisdom, or *gnānam*; one
who has received the qualities and wisdom of God by surrendering
to God, and, having received these, lives in a state of peace where
he sees all lives as equal; one who has attained the state of peace.

hadīth (A) In Islam, authenticated statements relating to the deeds and
utterances of the Prophet ☪. If the words or commands of Allah

were received directly by the Prophet Muhammad ⊕, it is known as a *hadīth qudsī*. Words of wisdom; discourse of wisdom. Sometimes *hadīth* can mean a story about the prophets.

hadīyah (A) Gift.

hajj (A) The holy pilgrimage to Mecca; the fifth obligatory duty *(fard)* in Islam. This duty must be done wearing the white shroud *(kafan)* of one who has died to the world. Before you undertake this pilgrimage you must share your wealth among the poor. If you have a wife and children, you must divide your wealth among them. True pilgrimage is to enter the state of dying before death. The inner desires must be surrendered and all of the self must die to make this pilgrimage.

Hajji Hajjiyar (A & T) A title used in Sri Lanka for someone who has gone on the holy pilgrimage of *hajj* more than one time.

Hajjiyar (A & T) A title used in Sri Lanka when someone has gone on the holy pilgrimage of *hajj*.

halāl (A) Permissible; those things that are permissible or lawful according to the commands of God and which conform to the word of God.

haqq (A) Truth; reality; the truth which is God; *al-Haqq*—one of the ninety-nine beautiful names of God.

harām (A) Forbidden; impermissible; that which is forbidden by truth, justice, and the commands of God. For those who are on the straight path, *harām* means all the evil things, actions, food, and dangers that can obstruct the path.

Hawwā' ⊕ (A) Eve.

hayāt (A) The plenitude of man's eternal life; the splendor of the completeness of life; the soul *(rūh)* of the splendor of man's life.

hayawān(s) (A) Beast.

'ibādat (A) Worship and service to the One God.

'ilm (A) Knowledge; divine knowledge; that secret knowledge, or light, that shines in the heart of the truly pious whereby one becomes enlightened.

imām (A) One who leads the congregation in the five-times prayer of Islam.

īmān (A) Absolute, complete, and unshakable faith, certitude, and determination that God alone exists; the complete acceptance by the heart that God is One.

Īmān-Islām (A) The state of the spotlessly pure heart which contains Allah's Holy Qur'an, His divine radiance, His divine wisdom, His truth, His prophets, His angels, and His laws. The pure heart which, having cut away all evil, takes on the power of that courageous determination called faith and stands shining in the resplendence of Allah.

When the resplendence of Allah is seen as the completeness within the heart of man, that is *Īmān-Islām*. When the complete unshakable faith of the heart is directed toward the One who is completeness; when that completeness is made to merge with the One who is completeness; when that heart communes with that One, trusts only in Him, and worships only Him, accepting only Him and nothing else as the only perfection and the only One worthy of worship—that is *Īmān-Islām*.

insān (A) Man; a human being. The true form of man is the form of Allah's qualities, actions, conduct, behavior, and virtues. The one who has realized the completeness of this form, having filled himself with these qualities, is truly an *insān*.

insān kāmil (A) A perfected, God-realized being; one who has realized Allah as his only wealth, cutting away all the wealth of the world and the wealth sought by the mind, one who has acquired God's qualities, performs his own actions accordingly, and contains himself within those qualities.

Islam (A) Spotless purity; the state of absolute purity; to accept the commands of God, His qualities, and His actions, and to establish that state within oneself. To cut away desire, to accept Him and know Him without the slightest doubt, and then to worship Him alone is Islam. To strengthen one's *īmān*; to accept *Lā ilāha ill-Allāhu* (There is nothing other than You, O God. Only You are Allah.) with absolute certitude, and to affirm this *kalimah*—that is the state of Islam. Also, the religion or creed of Islam.

Isrāfīl ☒ (A) Raphael, the archangel of air.

'Izrā'īl ☒ (A) Israel, the Angel of Death; the archangel of fire.

jahannam (A) Hell.

Jibrīl ☒ (A) Gabriel, the heavenly messenger who transmits divine wisdom; the archangel who brings the revelations of Allah. It is through Jibrīl ☒ that Allah conveyed the Qur'an to Prophet Muhammad ☒.

246 Die Before Death

Ka'bah (A) In the religion of Islam, the *Ka'bah* is both the most
important shrine of worship and the symbol of the unity of worship
of all believers. One of the five obligations *(furūd)* of Islam is the
pilgrimage *(hajj)* to the *Ka'bah.* It is a cube-like building in the
center of the mosque in Mecca. Rebuilt by Prophet Abraham (ﷺ)
and his son, the Prophet Ishmael (ﷺ), the *Ka'bah* subsequently
became filled with a multitude of idols. The Prophet Muhammad (ﷺ)
was commanded by God to cleanse the Holy House of all idols
and to restore its original purity and sanctity.

Within the human being, the *Kab'ah* represents the heart *(qalb)*,
the original source of prayer. It is the place in which a true man
meets God face to face. Like the outer *Ka'bah*, this sanctuary, too,
must be cleansed of idols and restored to its original purity as the
house in which God abides.

kafan (A) A cloth that is wound around a corpse.

kāfir (A) One who conceals Allah's truth; one who fails to live
according to Allah's qualities and virtues although being aware of
what Allah has commanded and forbidden; one who is ungrateful or
who rejects Allah after having awareness of the truth; one who
worships things as equal to Allah, falling under the power of his
base desires. Such a one hides the truth out of purely selfish
motives, turning the *qalb* into the form of darkness, falling prey to
the forces of satan, and acquiring the qualities of satan.

kālam (T) The time limit, the allotted duration for the life of each
creation.

Kali yuga (T) The present age, being the last of the four *yugas*, or
eons, of the world.

kalimah (A) The affirmation of faith—*Lā ilāha ill-Allāhu:* There is
nothing other than You, O God. Only You are Allah.

The recitation or remembrance of God which cuts away the
influence of the five elements (earth, fire, water, air, and ether),
washes away all the *karma* that has accumulated from the very
beginning until now, dispels the darkness, beautifies the heart, and
makes it resplend. The *kalimah* washes the body and the heart of
man and makes him pure, makes his wisdom emerge, and impels
that wisdom to know the self and God. *See also dhikr; Lā ilāha ill-
Allāhu.*

kamil (A) Perfect; perfect one.

Kārana Nabī (T & A) The Causal Prophet, Muhammad (ﷺ); all
creations came forth through Muhammad; Muhammad (ﷺ) is the last

of the line of prophets, the Final Prophet. But, he was there from the first, for Allah has said, "O Muhammad, I would not have created anything without you." That same beauty called *mīm* (the Arabic letter for 'm' which is shaped like a sperm) which came at the beginning also comes at the end as the beauty of Muhammad ﷺ. If something had not been there at the beginning, it will not come at the end. *See also mīm; Nabī.*

Karbalā' (A) When Allah ordered the Angel 'Izrā'īl ﷺ to take a handful of earth, from which Adam ﷺ was created, that handful of earth gathered from all four directions was placed in *Karbalā'*, the center of the eighteen thousand universes.

It is also a city located in Iraq, which throughout the ages has been a battlefield. It is where Husain ﷺ the son of 'Alī ﷺ, fought against his enemies and was killed. On a symbolic level, *Karbalā'* signifies the battlefield of the heart *(qalb)*.

karma (T) The inherited qualities formed at the time of conception; the qualities of the essence of the five elements; the qualities of the mind; the qualities of the connection to hell; the qualities and actions of the seventeen *purānas* which are: arrogance, *karma*, and *māyā*, or illusion; the three sons of *māyā (tārahan, singhan, and sūran)*, the six intrinsic evils of lust, anger, greed, attachment, bigotry, and envy, and the five acquired evils of intoxication, desire, theft, falsehood, and murder.

khair (A) That which is right or good; that which is acceptable to wisdom and to Allah, as opposed to *sharr*, that which is evil or bad.

khātim (A) A title of respect, commonly used in Sri Lanka. Lit. the Seal of Prophets; a name given to Muhammad ﷺ to designate that he was the Seal or Final Prophet to be sent by Allah.

kun (A) The word of the Lord meaning, "Be! Arise!" with which He caused all of everything to exist.

kursī (A) The gnostic eye; the eye of light; the center of the forehead where Allah's resplendence *(Nūr)* was impressed on Adam's ﷺ forehead. Lit. the "footstool" or seat of the resplendence of Allah.

Lā ilāha ill-Allāhu (A) There is nothing other than You, O God. Only You are Allah. To accept this with certitude, to strengthen one's determined faith *(īmān)*, and to affirm this *kalimah* is the state of Islam.

There are two aspects. *Lā ilāha* is the manifestation of creation *(sifāt)*. *Ill-Allāhu* is the essence *(dhāt)*. All that has appeared, all creation, belongs to *lā ilāha*. The name of the One who created all

that is *ill-Allāhu*. Lit. No god (is), except the One God. *See also*
kalimah; dhikr.

Lā ilāha ill-Allāhu Muhammadur-Rasūlullāh (A) There is nothing other
than You, O God. Only You are Allah and Muhammad is the
Messenger of God.

lakh (T) One hundred thousand.

lebbe (A) One who gives his life in service to God in a mosque and
performs all or certain duties within the mosque.

līlas (T) Sexual arts.

mahshar (A) The gathering on Judgment Day.

malak (A) (pl. *malā'ikat*) Angel.

mal'ūn (A) Accursed; rejected; a name attributed to satan.

mantra(s) (T) An incantation or formula; the recitation of a magic
word or set of words; sounds imbued with force or energy, through
constant repetition, but limited to the energy of the five elements.
(The *kalimah* is not a *mantra*.)

manu-Īsan (T) Man-God; man is God's secret and God is man's secret;
one who attains a high state of perfection will become a
representative of God, and it is through his qualities, actions, and
duties that God's qualities, actions, and duties can be seen and
understood.

maut (A) Death.

māyā (T) Illusion; the unreality of the visible world; the glitters seen
in the darkness of illusion; the 105 million glitters seen in the
darkness of the mind which result in 105 million rebirths. *Māyā* is
an energy, or *shakti*, which takes on various shapes, causes man to
forfeit his wisdom, and confuses and hypnotizes him into a state of
torpor. It can take many, many millions of hypnotic forms. If man
tries to grasp one of these forms with his intellect, although he sees
the form he will never catch it, for it will elude him by taking on
yet another form.

Mīkā'īl ☺ (A) Michael, the archangel of water.

Mi'rāj (A) The night journey of the Prophet Muhammad ☺ through
the heavens said to have taken place in the twelfth year of the
Prophet's ☺ mission on the twenty-seventh day of the month of
Rajab. During this event the divine order for five-times prayer was
given. Lit. an ascent.

mizān trās (A & T) God's scale. Lit. balancing scale.

muhaiyyan (A) Face; the beauty of the face.

muham (T) Face; the beauty of the face.

mu'min(s) (A) A true believer; one of absolute faith, certitude, and determination (*īmān*).

munivar(s) (T) One who performs elemental miracles (*siddhis*); a sage.

Munkar and Nakīr ☺ (A) The two angels who, in the grave, question the actions of every part of the body.

Mustafar-Rasūl ☺ (A) The Chosen Messenger ☺.

nabī(s) (A) (pl. *ambiyā'*) A prophet; one who has received direct inspiration by means of an angel or by the inspiration of the heart.

nafs or *nafs ammārah* (A) The self-nature, soul, spirit, or essence of a thing. In Sufism different levels of the *nafs* are delineated, from the lowest to the highest states of realization. The *nafs ammārah* describes the *nafs* at the lowest level, which compels a person to be motivated by base desires. It is known as the inciting *nafs*. Lit. personality; spirit; inclination or desire which goads or incites toward evil.

nasīb (A) Destiny or fate; share or portion.

nithānam (T) Balance.

nujumis (T) Astrologers.

nuqat (A) (sing. *nuqtah*) Dots (often used in this text to mean a singular dot); diacritical mark placed over or under certain Arabic letters to differentiate one from another.

Nūr (A) Light; the resplendence of Allah; the plenitude of the light of Allah which has the brilliance of a hundred million suns; the completeness of Allah's qualities. When the plenitude of all these becomes one and resplends as one, that is the *Nūr*—that is Allah's qualities and His beauty. It is the resplendent wisdom which is innate in man and can be awakened.

Nūr Muhammad (A) The beauty of the qualities and actions of the powers (*wilāyāt*) of Allah, the radiance of Allah's essence (*dhāt*) which shines within the resplendence of His truth. It was the light of Muhammad ☺ called *Nūr Muhammad* that was impressed upon the forehead of Adam ☺. Of the nine aspects of Muhammad ☺, *Nūr Muhammad* is that aspect which is the wisdom.

olis (T) Those who have realized the state of *īmān* (faith, certitude, and determination); those who have disappeared within the resplendence of Allah, shining and radiating without the least trace of fault or blemish.

pahuth arivu (T) Divine analytic wisdom; the sixth of the seven levels of wisdom, which cuts away the illusions of the elements and explains the truth of God; the *Qutbiyyat*; the atom within an atom in a man which cuts open and analyzes everything—what he sees, hears, feels, tastes, smells; what he intends, dreams, realizes; the heavens, the hells, and the plenitude of God. *See also Qutb, qutbiyyat.*

pūjā(s) (T) Ritual prayer or worship.

purānas (T) Stories, usually referring to the Hindu scriptures; mythologies; legends; epics. The stories of each religion can be described as *purānas*. Some were sent down as commandments from God, others were created through man's intelligence and senses, while still others were created by poets, usually as songs of praise depicting stories.

   Bawa Muhaiyaddeen ☺ speaks of the seventeen *purānas* within man as the qualities of arrogance, *karma*, and *māyā*; the three sons of *māyā* (*tārahan, singhan,* and *sūran*); lust, anger, miserliness, attachment, fanaticism, envy, intoxicants, obsession, theft, murder, and falsehood.

qabr (A) (sing. *qubūr*) Grave.

qada' (A) Fate or destiny.

al-qada' wal-qadar (A) Fate or destiny and the divine decree.

Qādir (A) God, the Powerful One; one of the ninety-nine names of God.

qalb (A) Heart; the heart within the heart of man; the innermost heart. Bawa Muhaiyaddeen ☺ explains that there are two states for the *qalb*. In one state the *qalb* is made up of four chambers which are earth, fire, air, and water—representing Hinduism, Fire Worship, Christianity, and Islam. Inside these four chambers is the second state, the flower of the *qalb* which is the divine qualities of God. This is the flower of grace (*rahmat*). God's fragrance exists within this inner *qalb*.

qiblah (A) The direction one faces in prayer; internally, it is the throne of God within the heart (*qalb*).

qismat (A) Perfect duty; doing good actions and acts of service. There is duty toward mankind, duty toward elders, and so many others, but if you can perform duty to Allah in addition to all these, that is even more exalted. If one does these duties with clarity, that is his fate or destiny. Lit. fate or destiny; to apportion to each what is due.

Qiyāmah (A) The standing forth; Day of Reckoning; Day of Questioning.

qudrat (A) Power; the power of God's grace and the qualities which control all other forces.

Qur'an (A) The words of God that were revealed to His Messenger, Prophet Muhammad ☾, those words that came from His Power are called the Qur'an; God's inner book of the heart; the light and lives of God's grace which came as the resonance from Allah; that which resonated from Him and became understood; that which never dies; that light and power which are His one hundred glorious names and His form (*sūrat*). He gives it life, and that is the *Nūr*, or the wisdom which explains. That is the Guru which is the light, and the *Rasūl* ☾. It is the beautiful light which has to be understood from inside.

Qutb(s) (A) Divine analytic wisdom; the wisdom which explains; that which measures the length and breadth of the seven oceans of the *nafs*, or base desires; that which awakens all the truths which have been destroyed and buried in the ocean of illusion (*māyā*); that which awakens true faith, certitude, and determination (*īmān*); that which gives explanations to life (*hayāt*); the state of purity as it existed in the beginning of creation (*awwal*); the grace of the essence of God (*dhāt*), which awakens the life (*hayāt*) of purity and transforms it into the divine vibration.

    Qutb is also a name which has been given to Allah. He can be addressed as *Yā Qutb* or *Yā Quddūs*, the Holy One. *Quddūs* is His power or miracle (*wilāyat*), while *Qutb* is His action. *Wilāyat* is the power of that action. Lit. axis; axle; pole; pivot; a title used for the great holy men of Islam.

Qutbiyyat (A) The wisdom of the *Qutb*; the sixth level of consciousness; divine analytic wisdom; the wisdom which explains the truth of God.

Qutbiyyat Nūr (A) A shortened form of *Nūrul-Qutbiyyat*. The light of the *Qutbiyyat*.

Rabb (ar-Rabb) (A) God; the Lord; the Creator and Protector.

Rabbul-'ālamīn (A) Lord of all the universes.

ar-Rahīm (A) The Most Compassionate; the Sustainer and Redeemer; one of the ninety-nine beautiful names of God. He is the One who is full of endless compassion for all lives. *See also Bismillāhir-Rahmānir-Rahīm.*

ar-Rahmān (A) The Most Gracious, Most Merciful; one of the ninety-nine beautiful names of Allah. He is the King. He is the Nourisher, the One who gives food. He is the Compassionate One. He is the One who protects the creations. He is the Beneficent One.

rahmat (A) God's grace; His mercy; His forgiveness and compassion; His benevolence; His wealth. To all creations, He is the wealth of life (*hayāt*) and the wealth of absolute faith, certitude, and determination (*īmān*). All the good things that we receive from God are His *rahmat*. That is the wealth of God's plenitude. Everything that is within God is *rahmat*, and if He were to give that grace, that would be an undiminishing, limitless wealth.

Rahmatul-'ālamīn (A) The Mercy and Compassion of all the universes; the One who gives everything to all His creations.

Rajab (A) A month of the Hijrah calendar, during which *Mi'rāj* (the night journey of Muhammad �;) is commemorated.

Raqīb and 'Atīd �; (A) The two recording angels on your right and left shoulders.

Rasūl �; (A) Allah's Messenger, Muhammad �;, is His essence (*dhāt*), the resplendence that emerged from His effulgence, shining radiantly as His Messenger �;. Muhammad �;, the manifestation of that resplendence, discourses on the explanations of luminous wisdom which he imparts to Allah's creations. He is the one who begs for truth from Allah and intercedes with prayers for all of Allah's creations and for his followers. Therefore, Allah has anointed His *Rasūl*, the Prophet Muhammad �;, with the title: *The Messenger who is the savior for both worlds.*

The word *rasūl* can be used to refer to any of Allah's apostles or messengers. *See also rasūl.*

rasūl(s) (A) Apostle or messenger; one who has wisdom, faith in God, and good qualities; one who behaves with respect and dignity toward his fellow man. A *rasūl* is one who has completely accepted only God and has rejected everything else; one who has accepted God's divine words, His qualities and actions, and puts them into practice. Those who from time immemorial have given the divine laws of God to the people; one who has such a connection with God is called a prophet (nabī) or a rasūl. Yā Rasūl is a name given to the Prophet Muhammad ⊕ when one calls upon him.

Rasūlullāh ⊕ (A) The Messenger of Allah; a title used for Prophet Muhammad ⊕.

Ridwān and Mālik ☺ (A) Ridwān ☺ is the angel who guards the entrance to heaven. Mālik ☺ is the angel in charge of the punishment in hell.

rizq (A) Nourishment; food; sustenance; that which is given as true food and provision by ar-Razzāq, the Provider.

rūh (A) The soul; the light ray of God; the light of God's wisdom. Bawa Muhaiyaddeen ⊕ explains that rūh also means life (hayāt). Out of the six kinds of lives it is the light life, the ray of the light of the resplendence of Allah, the Nūr, which does not die. It does not disappear; it is the truth. The other five lives appear and disappear. That which exists forever without death is the soul. It is Allah's grace (rahmat) which has obtained the wealth of the imperishable treasure of all three worlds (mubārakāt).

Rūqā'īl ☺ (A) The angel of protection.

sabūr (A) Inner patience; to go within patience, to accept it, to think and reflect within it. Sabūr is that patience deep within patience which comforts, soothes, and alleviates mental suffering.
    Yā Sabūr—one of the ninety-nine names of Allah. God, who in a state of limitless patience, is always forgiving the faults of His created beings and continuing to protect them.

sadaqah (A) Charity; contributions to the poor; the third obligatory duty of Islam which requires Muslims to give a certain percentage of their income to the needy and poor. True charity is to recognize the lives of others to be as valuable as one's own and to comfort and care for them as one would for oneself.

salām(s) (A) Peace; the peace of God. Greetings! When one says salām to another, it means in God's name or in the presence of God, may both of us become one without any division; both of us are in a state of unity, a state of peace.

salawāt (A) (sing. salāt) Prayers; blessings; glorification. The practice of praising, glorifying, invoking peace upon Allah, the Rasūl ⊕, the prophets, and the angels.
    The praise that you offer to Allah, the Rasūl ⊕, and the heavenly

beings comes back to you as your own treasure, your own wealth. The *salāms* and *salawāt* you offer come back to you and light up your own face and heart. This is the reason that the *salawāt* is considered to be something very exalted.

sayyid (A) Descendant of Prophet Muhammad ☮.

shaitān (A) Satan.

shakti(s) (T) Force; energy.

shakūr (A) Gratitude; contentment; contentment arising from gratitude; the state within the inner patience known as *sabūr*, that which is stored within the treasure chest of patience.
    Yā Shakūr—one of the ninety-nine beautiful names of Allah. To have *shakūr* with the help of the One who is *Yā Shakūr* is true *shakūr*.

sharr (A) That which is wrong, bad, or evil, as opposed to *khair*, that which is good.

sheikh or *shaikh* (A) Teacher of divine wisdom; the catalyst or stimulant who activates the wisdom of his disciple. The true sheikh is that agent which separates the whey from the water in the milk, which transforms the whey into curd, and the curd into buttermilk, which separates the top cream from the buttermilk and brings forth clarified ghee from the buttermilk. The sheikh pleads, exhorts, and clarifies. He reveals and teaches. He induces the disciple to understand and realize for himself, and thus he melts the very being of the disciple in order that the disciple may come to see that for which he seeks. This is the sole purpose for which the sheikh appears to his disciple. Used in the text as an English word.

Shīva (T) The aspect of God worshiped by Hindus as the Transformer.

sifāt (A) (sing. *sifat*) That which arose from the word "Be!" (*Kun!*); all that has come into being as form. Depending on the context, the word *sifāt* may mean the creations or manifestations of God or the attributes of God.

Sirātul-Mustaqīm (A) The straight path; the straight path of righteousness.

sirr (A) Secret; the secret of Allah.

sitthar (T) One who performs *sitthis*, or elemental miracles.

Subhānahu wa ta'ālā or *Allāhu subhānahu wa ta'ālā* (A) Allah, glory and exaltedness is His! A spontaneous outpouring of love from a believer's heart upon hearing or uttering the name Allah.

sūrat (A) Form or shape, such as the form of man (spelled with the Arabic letter *sād*).

sūrat (A) A chapter of the Qur'an (spelled with the Arabic letter *sīn*). Lit. a row or series.

Sūratul-Fātihah (A) The opening chapter of the Qur'an; the inner form of man; the clarity of understanding the four elements of the body (earth, fire, water, and air), and the realization of the self and of Allah within. The *Sūratul-Fātihah* is recited at the beginning of every prayer. Within man is the *Sūratul-Fātihah*, and within the *Sūratul-Fātihah* is the inner form of man. If we split open that form, we can see within it Allah's words, His qualities, His actions, His three thousand divine attributes, and His ninety-nine powers (*wilāyāt*). That is the inner form of man (*sūratul-insān*).

    The *Sūratul-Fātihah* must be split open with wisdom to see all these within. It must be opened by the ocean of divine knowledge (*bahrul-'ilm*). Opening his heart (*qalb*), opening his form (*sūrat*) and looking within, having his own form looking at his own form—that is the *Sūratul-Fātihah*. What is recited on the outside is the *Al-hamdu Sūrat*. The outer meaning is on the first level of spiritual ascendance (*sharī'at*); the inner meaning relates to the essence (*dhāt*). *Fātihah* means literally to open out. It is opening the heart and looking within.

sūratul-insān (A) The inner form of man. The inner form of man, or *sūratul-insān*, is the Qur'an and is linked together by the twenty-eight letters. This form (*sūrat*) is the *Ummul-Qur'ān*, the source of the Qur'an. It is the Qur'an in which the revelations are revealed. The sounds of the Qur'an exist in this body as secrets and are made to resonate through wisdom, through the Messenger of Allah, Prophet Muhammad ☺, and through the angels and heavenly beings. They can be seen in the letters which compose the *sūratul-insān*.

Sūratul-Qur'ān (A) The inner form of the Qur'an; the body made of the twenty-eight Arabic letters. Man's *sūrat* has been formed by the Qur'an; that is the *sūratul-Qur'ān*.

Sūratur-Rahmān (A) A chapter of the Qur'an.

Sūrat Yā Sīn (A) A chapter of the Qur'an often referred to as the heart of the Qur'an.

talāq (A) Divorce.

tārahan, singhan, and *sūran* (T) The three sons of illusion *(māyā)*. *Tārahan* is the trench or the pathway for the sexual act, the birth canal or vagina. *Singhan* is the arrogance present at the moment when the semen is ejaculated *(karma)*. It is the quality of the lion. *Sūran* is the illusory images of the mind enjoyed at the moment of ejaculation. It is all the qualities and energies of the mind.

tasbīh (A) Glorification of God; offering prayers of praise.

tattwa(s) (A) The strength or power that is inherent in the qualities of the creations, manifesting through the action of each respective quality. While jinns, demons, and ghosts have thirty-six *tattwas,* man has ninety-six, and through these he can control everything.

taubah or *at-taubah* (A) Repentance; to ask God's pardon for sins and errors, to turn away from them, and to vow not to commit them again.

tawakkul or *tawakkul-'alallāh* (A) Absolute trust in God; surrender to God; handing over to God the entire responsibility for everything. *Al-Wakīl* is one of the ninety-nine beautiful names of Allah: the Trustee, the Guardian.

thānam (T) Surrender.

toluhai (T) The performance of prayer where one remembers only God to the exclusion of everything else. Also refers to the five-times prayer of Islam.

'ulamā' (A) (sing. *'ālim*) Teachers; learned ones; scholars.

'Umar Ibnul-Khattāb ☺ (A) The second caliph and a father-in-law to the Prophet ☺. At first he was violently opposed to Muhammad ☺, but later heard his sister reciting part of the Qur'an and was overcome. Going directly to Muhammad ☺, he professed his belief in Allah and His Prophet ☺.

ummat (A) Followers of the Prophet Muhammad ☺.

Ummul-Qur'ān (A) The 'source' or 'mother' of the Qur'an. It is used commonly to refer to the *Sūratul-Fātihah,* or the opening chapter of the Qur'an. It is said that within the 124 letters of the *Sūratul-Fātihah* is contained the meaning of the entire Qur'an. It is often used to denote the eternal source of all the revelations to all of the prophets and is also known as the *Ummul-Kitāb* (the mother, or source, of the book). This is a divine, indestructible tablet on which all is recorded. This is the silent Qur'an which exists as a mystery within the heart *(qalb)* of each person.

unarchi (T) Awareness; the second level of consciousness.

vanakkam (T) True prayer.

al-Wakīl (A) The Trustee.

waqt(s) (A) Time of prayer. In the religion of Islam there are five specified *waqts*, or times of prayer, each day. But truly, there is only one *waqt*. That is the prayer that never ends, wherein one is in direct communication with God and one is merged in God.

wilāyat (A) (pl. *wilāyāt*) God's power; that which has been revealed and manifested through God's actions; the miraculous names and actions of God; the powers of His attributes through which all creations came into existence.

Yā (A) The vocative 'O'. An exclamation of praise; a title of greatness and glory.

Yā Rabbal-'ālamīn (A) O Ruler of the universes! The Creator who nourishes and protects all of His creations forever.

Yahweh (Hebrew) God; Jehovah.

Yaman (Sanskrit) The Angel of Death in the Hindu tradition.

yuga(s) (T) An age; one of the four ages of the world. According to M. R. Bawa Muhaiyaddeen ۞ the world has been in existence for 200 million years and is divided into four *yugas* of 50 million years each.

INDEX

BOOKS BY
M. R. BAWA MUHAIYADDEEN

Truth & Light: brief explanations

Songs of God's Grace

The Divine Luminous Wisdom That Dispels the Darkness

Wisdom of the Divine (Vols. 1, 2, 3, 4, 5)

The Guidebook to the True Secret of the Heart (Vols. 1, 2)

God, His Prophets and His Children

Four Steps to Pure Iman

The Wisdom of Man

A Book of God's Love

*My Love You My Children:
101 Stories for Children of All Ages*

Come to the Secret Garden: Sufi Tales of Wisdom

The Golden Words of a Sufi Sheikh

The Tasty, Economical Cookbook (Vols. 1, 2)

Sheikh and Disciple

Maya Veeram or The Forces of Illusion

Asma'ul-Husna: The 99 Beautiful Names of Allah

Islam and World Peace: Explanations of a Sufi

A Mystical Journey

Questions of Life—Answers of Wisdom

Treasures of the Heart: Sufi Stories for Young Children

A Song of Muhammad ⊕

Gems of Wisdom series—
Vol. 1: The Value of Good Qualities
Vol. 2: Beyond Mind and Desire
Vol. 3: The Innermost Heart
Vol. 4: Come to Prayer

A Contemporary Sufi Speaks—
To Teenagers and Parents
On the Signs of Destruction
On Peace of Mind
On the True Meaning of Sufism
On Unity: The Legacy of the Prophets
The Meaning of Fellowship

Foreign Language Publications—
Ein Zeitgenössischer Sufi Spricht über Inneren Frieden
(A Contemporary Sufi Speaks on Peace of Mind—German Translation)

Deux Discours tirés du Livre
L'Islam et la Paix Mondiale: Explications d'un Soufi
(Two Discourses from the Book
Islam & World Peace: Explanations of a Sufi—French Translation)

For free catalog or book information call:
(215) 879-8604

The central branch of the Bawa Muhaiyaddeen Fellowship is located in Philadelphia, PA. The Fellowship serves as a meeting house and as a reservoir of people and materials for all who are interested in the teachings of M. R. Bawa Muhaiyaddeen.

For information, write or call:

The Bawa Muhaiyaddeen Fellowship
5820 Overbrook Avenue
Philadelphia, Pennsylvania 19131

―――――

Telephone: (215) 879-6300
or
(215) 879-8604
(24 hour answering machine)

―――――

E-Mail Address:
info@bmf.org

URL Web Address:
http://www.bmf.org